COMMON
DENOMINATORS
FOR SUCCESS

COMMON DENOMINATORS FOR SUCCESS

7 Universal Formulas to Get the Results You Want

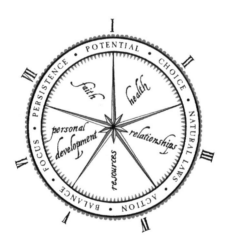

KENNY J. ANDERSON

Library of Congress Control Number: 2010915578

ISBN: 978-0-615-39002-4

Direct inquiries to
www.kennyjanderson.com

First Edition
14 13 12 11 10   5 4 3 2 1

Text edited by Katie Newbold
Designed by Vance Hawkins

Printed and bound in the U.S.

*To my wife, Rebecca, and our four children
for their unconditional love and support,
and for making life a joyous experience;
and to my wonderful parents for
teaching me the lasting value
of correct principles.*

Contents

1   Introduction

17   Unlimited Potential: Formula 1
   Within each of us lies unlimited potential.
   The only limitations in life are those we place upon ourselves.

41   Power to Choose: Formula 2
   Success is not a matter of chance but a matter of choice.

55   Recipe for Success: Formula 3
   Results stem from natural laws adhered to or broken.

73   Action = Results: Formula 4
   Wisdom is knowledge applied.

95   Balance: Formula 5
   Real success is the consistent application of correct principles
   in every aspect of life.

145   In the Zone: Formula 6
   Focus is achieved as we overcome roadblocks to success.

163   Breakout: Formula 7
   A lifetime commitment to success is found in the persistent
   pursuit of excellence.

179   Blueprint for Success

193   Acknowledgments

195   About the Author

Introduction

During the early production stages of this book, my editor asked what set my program apart from others and what qualified me to talk on this subject. For years I consulted people and companies on the diversification of their wealth and assets. Although I enjoyed being a stockbroker and recognize that showing people the best way to invest their money is beneficial, I've come to realize that the greater need is for people to diversify not only their financial portfolios but their *life* portfolios as well. Knowing how to invest in our lives is hands down the most common need of everyone I've associated with and the only way to find total success. All money diversifications are in vain if people's lives are in chaos. This is why we tend to see that many wealthy, famous people are still unhappy and often have their priorities backward. To truly be successful, we must have a proper balance and build our lives on a solid foundation of correct principles.

For more than twenty years I've searched for a formula that would fuel success in every aspect of life, from health to personal development to relationships. This has been my passion, primarily because I want to motivate others and help them understand that the price we must pay to obtain our dreams is worth it and that we can achieve those aspirations. Most people can't be reached and don't see a need until they are in dire straits. Some choose not to be healthy until they suffer a heart attack; others steer clear of talking about life dreams because of regret or fear of failure. My main desire in writing this book and creating this program for change is to show people—people like you and me—that they can't afford to give up on their dreams. The consequences of an unfulfilled, unhappy, and unsuccessful life are far too painful to bear. I think now, more than any other time in history, we need hope. We need to dream again. We need to consider all that is possible and then use the tools I provide through this program to make those dreams happen.

Through my own trial and error, successes and failures, I've discovered that there are common denominators for total success that can produce dramatic results if we apply them in all areas of our lives. I call them *common denominators* for success because no matter where you go in the world, if a person applies these principles to their lives in pursuit of honest desires, they will experience success time after time, regardless of their background, beliefs, or financial circumstances. I know these are common denominators for success because I've not only experienced them at work in my own life, but I've seen their results in the lives of those around me. These common denominators are broken into Seven Formulas for Success—formulas because their effectiveness is evident only when we apply all their components simultaneously and properly. Learning the Seven Formulas for Success is a lifelong pursuit—a quest to improve ourselves and to achieve a fullness of life—so there's no better time to start learning than now.

When I say that now's the best time to start this program, I'm directing my advice at everyone, no matter what stage of life you're in—whether you're the person who's given up on life or you're the everyday person trying to find balance and satisfaction in your daily routine. Maybe you're the person stuck in a rut, wanting to make a change, or the elite athlete trying to master his game, or the businesswoman attempting to climb the corporate ladder or start your own business. This program works for those who are struggling with their weight, or seeking purpose and meaning in life, or beside themselves with the demands of a family and desperately need balance. This program will work for a company wanting to increase sales or for a firm wanting to create a more cohesive environment among its employees. This program and the Seven Formulas for Success will provide any individual or company with a blueprint to successfully reach their potential and attain their dreams, whatever they may be.

The Seven Formulas for Success are universal truths that govern our choices. They consist of the following:

Formula 1: *Within each of us lies unlimited potential. The only limitations in life are those we place upon ourselves.*

Formula 2: *Success is not a matter of chance but a matter of choice.*

Formula 3: *Results stem from natural laws adhered to or broken.*

Formula 4: *Wisdom is knowledge applied.*

Formula 5: *Real success is the consistent application of correct principles in every aspect of life.*

Formula 6: *Focus is achieved as we overcome roadblocks to success.*

Formula 7: *A lifetime commitment to success is found in the persistent pursuit of excellence.*

The key to true and ultimate success in life is the proper application of these universal truths in every aspect of life. Even though we may not share the same culture, race, or religion, you and I have the same fundamental needs and value the same aspects of life. There are five areas that comprise our common values and give us a framework for determining and measuring our success:

1. Faith
2. Relationships
3. Personal Development
4. Health
5. Resources (Time and Money)

If we apply the seven formulas to our five core values, we will live a balanced life and achieve total success.

Life is composed of natural laws, which when adhered to can bring about profoundly effective results; however, when we ignore these laws, the consequences we yield can be painful and unbearable at times. Just as every aspect of our lives is affected by the law of gravity or any of the other laws of physics, similarly there are other laws that determine the outcome of our choices, such as the laws of health. One of those laws, for example, is that if you eat less calories than you burn, you will lose weight. Sometimes we don't know or understand the laws and therefore, we don't know how to tap into the promised results. Other times we may find success in one aspect of life but have a difficult time implementing that success in other areas. The key is to keep seeking to know the formulas for a successful, balanced life.

Over the course of my life I've found great passion in studying formulas for success. By observing life through this lens and having experienced my own share of successes and failures, I've come to the conclusion that all success is achieved when obedience to a law is received. This may sound easy, but it's not—we must pay the price through hard work and sacrifice. Short-term sacrifices bring long-term results.

There are books on the market today that claim that people can achieve results by just thinking about what they desire without any action of their own. This would be like trying to drive a car without an engine or skydiving without a parachute. We must take action and do our part if we are to achieve our desired results. In addition, other books about success generally focus on one aspect of life, like time management or personal development, disregarding the need for an all-inclusive balance that is required to obtain total fulfillment, total success, and total satisfaction. I find that these books contain some correct concepts but lack the substance and practical implementation necessary to really help us succeed in our day-to-day lives.

After reading this book and learning how to apply the seven underlying formulas, you will see positive results in every aspect of your life, from relationships to financial quests to health. If you follow the formulas and guidelines I lay out in this book, I assure you that your life will be full and that no matter what obstacles block your path, you will be triumphant. I have studied, implemented, and discussed these principles for more than twenty years as a student, stockbroker, husband, father, entrepreneur, and the list could go on. The formulas not only work, they work in every aspect of life! Once you learn these seven formulas, there is no limit to what you can accomplish.

Seven Formulas for Success

Formula 1: Unlimited Potential
Within each of us lies unlimited potential. The only limitations in life are those we place upon ourselves.

Do you ever feel like there are not enough hours in a day to accomplish everything you need to? Do you feel like you want to break the bands that limit you and burst through the ceiling of opportunity but just don't know how? Do you feel like you do pretty well in some aspects of life, but you can't seem to succeed in other areas? Rest assured that when you begin to understand how to apply these seven formulas to the five core values of your life, there will be no stopping you!

So start with the first formula by believing that there is no end to your potential.

Each one of us literally has an unlimited capacity to succeed. We are kept down only by our own doubts. When we understand that we have unlimited potential within us and we are in charge, we will have the faith and understanding to begin the journey to success. Now, we've all heard the saying, "What you believe, you can achieve," and maybe it makes us roll our eyes and tune out because it's unrealistic, but the fact is, we literally will become what we think. There's a universal formula that governs this process, which states, "Within each of us lies unlimited potential. The only limitations in life are those we place upon ourselves." When we tap into the power that comes from its positive application, we can soar to heights that we have only dreamed of and this book will show you how.

We've all been knocked down in our lives, but it's time to get up and get going. There is too much for you to do and too much life ready to be lived. It doesn't matter where you've been; it only matters where you are today and where you're going tomorrow. Put the past in perspective and learn from it; visualize the future ahead and prepare for it; and focus on the present and live it! Our potential is limitless, and as we begin to expand our vision, we will be en route to achieving our full potential.

Formula 2: Power to Choose
Success is not a matter of chance but a matter of choice.

Once we realize that our potential is limitless, we understand that our lives are a product of our choices and that we ultimately determine our outcome. We must take responsibility for our lives and determine to live in a way that will invite the fruits of success. What sets us apart from each other is the attitude we choose and the responsibility we take for our thoughts, words, and actions. The truth is that the thoughts we entertain will ultimately become our words and actions, and therefore we must choose wisely in order to reach our full potential.

Many of us blame others for our unfavorable circumstances instead of taking responsibility for ourselves. When we cast blame on others, we give up the ability to change our own lives, and we empower others to control who we are and to steal our dreams. No one is responsible for who you are except for you. Until we realize this, we set ourselves up for disappointment and despair.

The ability to choose lets us all stand as equals without excuses. This is where real life is realized, where true greatness evolves, and where our ability to accomplish our dreams comes together. Everyday heroes rise above their circumstances of life, and instead of blaming or excusing their failures, they take charge and make their lives into something prolific. Now is the time to take charge of your life and begin realizing those dreams that are in front of you. Anything is possible, and your dreams are just a choice away.

Formula 3: Recipe for Success
Results stem from natural laws adhered to or broken.

As we go through life there are certain principles that we must learn. Just like the law of gravity, all situations are governed by natural laws that yield an outcome. Make no mistake that the law will claim its prize; the question is whether or not we will receive the reward or the consequence of it. If we look closely we will find that all aspects of life have a recipe for success. For instance, if we want to become financially independent, we must spend less than we make. This sounds simple, but simple truths and principles are what drive success. It's not the principle that's tough; it's our ability to follow the principle that requires discipline and hard work. Sometimes we attempt to buck the system in order to shortcut the path to success. While we may try a shortcut and experience an illusion of results, the outcome will never be long lasting enough to sustain our ultimate goal.

Everything in this universe follows laws and the only way to get lasting results is by obeying those laws, but many times we want the results without paying the price. So instead of eating nutritiously and exercising, which we all know is a sure foundation for successful results, we shortcut the law by taking pills or injecting our bodies with needles, having the false illusion that we can gain the same lasting results. We may experience some short-term results, leading us to believe that the shortcut will permanently substitute unnecessary work and pain. Although trendy diets and fabulous stories can be compelling, the truth is that the formulas for success as they pertain to health cannot and will not be fooled. There is no shortcut to success. If we want to achieve our greatest desires in life, we must follow the natural laws and apply the formulas.

Since Formula 3 states that results stem from natural laws adhered to or broken, we know that the key to achieving success is to search out these natural laws and follow their instructions. This sure formula will get us the results we are looking for and allow us to break through to our ultimate potential in life. If we look closely, these correct principles can be found all around us. We must take the time to listen and learn from our own experiences and from those of others, and to then look for patterns and apply the knowledge we gain.

Formula 4: Action = Results
Wisdom is knowledge applied.

Once we have the formulas for success, we must apply them into our lives—knowledge without application means nothing. An engineer can learn useful formulas for building structures, but until he puts that knowledge into action, it serves no purpose and provides no value to him or those around him. Applied knowledge, which I call wisdom, is what unlocks the gates of success.

As we increase in wisdom, it is easier for us to recognize the universal laws and correct principles in the world around us. One such example is the *WBDA Principle*, which is the acronym for: "Want it. Believe it. Do it. Achieve it." If you want something badly enough, know that it is based on correct principles (remember, no short cuts), believe that you can accomplish it, and apply the steps of action, you will achieve it! Sounds simple, yet so often we are not willing to pay the price to receive the reward.

In order to apply the WBDA Principle and diversify our lives, we categorize our personal goals under the five core values—faith, relationships, personal development, health, and resources. We divide up our goals this way to avoid having too many of them in one area of life or not enough in another. We then contemplate our greatest desires and determine exactly why we want them, how we're going to achieve them, and when we're going to make time for them in our schedule. Establishing an organized plan gives us focus, making us more likely to follow through with our good intentions.

Formula 5: Balance

Real success is the consistent application of correct principles in every aspect of life.

Balance is a needed component in our lives. Many of us experience great success and joy in one aspect of life but come up wanting in other areas. For example, someone may have a wonderful family life and work at the job of their dreams, and yet suffer the ill effects of poor health. I have found that we can apply the same principles of success to every aspect of life regardless of the category. People who successfully manage their time in business can use this same skill to spend quality time with their family. The key is to focus your efforts on being 100 percent in that moment at that time. This success in time management can be duplicated just as well in health, finances, and any other aspect of life. Thus a successful life of ultimate fulfillment is comprised of correct principles applied again and again to all aspects of life.

Balance provides the real opportunity for us to unleash the full capacity within ourselves. In chapter 5 we will spend a considerable amount of time discussing examples that show the value of balance in our lives. As you discover what you are capable of, take responsibility for your choices, learn the formulas for success, and apply them into every aspect of your life, you will be on your way to a healthier, more balanced life.

Formula 6: In the Zone

Focus is achieved as we overcome roadblocks to success.

As we head down the path of life, focusing on the end goal should be our priority because along the way we will inevitably encounter roadblocks to success. These roadblocks can come in the form of fear, doubt, procrastination, excuses, and a myriad of other distractions that can detour our attention from what we really want. These roadblocks to success are very real, and if we don't account for them, we can be knocked off balance and end up succumbing to a pitfall. While we all will encounter obstacles in life, our ability to focus on what we ultimately want will allow us to move past these distractions and drive us successfully forward to what we really want.

A vital weapon in overcoming roadblocks to success and living in the moment is our ability to focus. We are most effective when we are positively directing our thoughts, words, actions, and energies to that which we want to accomplish. By surrounding ourselves with what is of greatest value and applying the seven formulas found in this book, we can give 100 percent attention to the task before us and be completely in the zone. When we learn to direct our attention and energies to being our best at what we are doing in that moment, we increase our chances for success.

Formula 7: Breakout

A lifetime commitment to success is found in the persistent pursuit of excellence.

This brings us to our final formula for powerful change, which I call *breakout*. Years ago I spent a considerable amount of time as a stockbroker and there discovered the characteristics of successful stocks. Day after day I would study thousands of graphs, trying to determine a successful formula that would achieve great results for my clients. I came to some interesting conclusions about the fundamental and technical data gathered from these successful companies and found strikingly valuable and similar parallels to human behavior.

When stocks begin to approach their threshold or all-time high, if they do not have enough momentum, they tend to fall back into some of the typical and historical trends of performance. Each of us also reaches a threshold, where we are so close to breaking out into new territory, but when we are just about to experience a breakout, we fall back into mediocrity and settle for what we consider to be "life as good as it gets."

Breaking out means aspiring and reaching our ultimate pinnacle of achievement. It means firing up all cylinders and taking charge of our lives, not settling for mediocrity. It means establishing a lifelong commitment to excellence and enduring as many upsets as it takes us to reach our goal. All of us want to enjoy the best things in life, but when we give up before the finish or stop believing we can ever attain them, we begin to make excuses of why life is not so great. The truth is that we *can* achieve those dreams we have always cherished. We can commit to excellence, and with perseverance and consistent hard work, we will experience a breakout.

If you will live the principles talked about in this book and apply the Seven Formulas for Success, you will discover a road map that will lead you to your desired location. The principles taught in this book have existed since the beginning of time and successful people in all facets of life, all cultures, and all eras of time have applied them and seen their powerful results—they are the common denominators for success. These seven formulas as well as all other natural laws can be implemented to improve your faith, relationships, personal development, health, and resources (time and money). True success and complete balance will come as you learn to apply correct principles to the five core values of life.

Blueprint for Success

Having established our five universal core values, we now solidify their significance in our lives by condensing them into a blueprint for success. You'll read more about this blueprint in chapter 8, but it is made up of action points found throughout each chapter that help us apply the seven formulas to our lives. Some of these action points are, for example, making a success journal, creating "as if" statements, and setting short- and long-term goals according to the WBDA Principle. This blueprint for success will act as a map to help us follow through on our goals and remind us what is most important in our lives. By establishing set guidelines to live by, we are more prepared to steer clear of unnecessary detours and avoid time-robbing pitfalls. Look around you in the world today and assess if we could use a blueprint of core values to guide our decisions. As a whole we suffer from a record number of broken relationships, soaring instances of depression and suicide, countless health issues including obesity and diabetes even in children, and widespread financial turmoil. It is without question that we all need a personalized blueprint to keep us focused on our goals and help us implement formulas for success into our everyday lives.

Common Denominators for Lasting Results

My passion for life has become a quest to learn the common denominators for success in order to achieve a healthy and balanced life, and help others do the same. I've found universally, regardless of race, gender, religion, or culture, that those who have properly applied correct principles to their lives have gotten lasting results and fulfilled their dreams. And it didn't matter if they were applying the principles to family or career, health or hobbies, the results were lasting. Those who are truly successful in every aspect of life have discovered that these formulas for success can unlock prosperity, and they are now reaping the ongoing rewards.

The things that you are doing now to reach your goals may not be producing lasting results because your actions aren't based on correct principles or timeless formulas for success. If you are frustrated and feel like your efforts are taking you nowhere, evaluate your methods and take note of what's working and what's not. I promise you that if you give up the quick fixes and shortcuts, and begin to implement the Seven Formulas for Success, you will ultimately find complete balance, lasting health, and real happiness.

If you are consistent, the Seven Formulas for Success can unlock the barriers that are keeping you from reaching your full potential. Once you learn these seven formulas, you will be able to apply them to your blueprint for success to reaffirm and strengthen your core values. With this newfound knowledge and confidence, you will be ready to move forward and reach your ultimate potential. It's time to dream again—your potential is right in front of you. Put the past in perspective and learn from it; visualize the future ahead and prepare for it; and focus on the present and live it!

Formula 1:
Unlimited Potential

Within each of us lies unlimited potential.
The only limitations in life are those we place upon ourselves.

Expand Your Vision of What Is Possible

What kind of life can you imagine for yourself? Do you believe that your days really can be happy and full? Have your dreams been extinguished by failure or disappointment? Have your hopes been stunted by others? Have you stopped dreaming because the dream seems unreachable or too difficult to obtain? As a result of forgotten hopes and dreams, has life lost some luster and excitement? If you have ever felt any of these emotions, I would challenge you to dream again. Don't give up and don't lose hope, because in reality you have enormous potential. Chances are the only person in your way of realizing that potential is you. Get out of your own way and tap into the reservoir of potential that awaits you.

Take for example the story of businessman John W. Nordstrom, who in 1887, at the age of sixteen, arrived in America from Sweden with only five dollars in his pocket. Unable to even speak English, John believed he could make his dreams a reality. Overcoming insurmountable odds, Nordstrom created a retail giant from the ground up, starting with a shoe store in downtown Seattle and then expanding into a nationwide fashion retail chain known as Nordstrom. This thriving company is recognized today as an industry leader and is legendary for its exceptional service and quality. John Nordstrom was not held back by supposed limitations, but rather he believed in himself and knew he could succeed.

Then there's the story of Harland Sanders, who at the age of sixty-five was virtually broke. With two possessions to his name—a car and a recipe for chicken—he overcame incredible barriers to found world-famous Kentucky Fried Chicken, serving more than twelve million customers daily in more than 109 countries and territories around the globe. Colonel Sanders believed in his unlimited capacity to succeed and would not be denied his dream.

Oftentimes our perceived limitations stop us from realizing our dreams. How we view a situation or a trial becomes our reality. If we see difficulty at every turn of life, then we will have difficulties. On the other hand, if we view adversity as an opportunity to learn and gain strength, then that is what we will gain. We are stunted only by our own limiting beliefs. We have the ability to be stronger than our perceived limitations and expand our mind to see the bigger picture of life.

We can do so much and live so well if we will begin to expand our vision of the potential within us. We must realize that the challenges of life prepare us to become our best selves.

Our potential is not restricted by what happens to us in life, but by our limiting beliefs of what we think we can do. When we realize that no matter what life may throw at us, we still control how we respond, we start to see the unlimited capacity within us.

As we enlarge our vision and see our true potential, we grow in our ability to tap into that reservoir within us. A successful life is not just for extraordinary people. A successful life is achieved by ordinary people with an extraordinary realization that their potential is limitless. We do not need to be held to a life of our own narrow beliefs—we can dream bigger than our perceived weaknesses and recognize that our abilities are limitless. We have the opportunity to enlarge our vision of what is possible.

Five Core Values

By realizing we have limitless potential, it is clear that we can achieve whatever we want in life if we follow the seven formulas laid out in this book. Some people may dream of starting their own business while others long to travel the world. Maybe you'd love a luxurious home or nice car while others want to be physically fit. Our desires may vary greatly from person to person, but there are a few core values we all treasure, regardless of our upbringing, belief system, gender, or ethnicity.

1. Faith
2. Relationships
3. Personal Development
4. Health
5. Resources (Time and Money)

The first of the five core values is faith. No matter what faith you claim, all of us have a belief system. You may have faith in a higher power that directs you and gives you hope and purpose, or you may fundamentally have faith that the sun will rise in the east and set in the west, but faith is faith. Maybe you believe in your abilities to accomplish your goals because of faith in a divine entity or faith in your own preparedness or innate capabilities. Or maybe it's a combination of both for you. Regardless what your higher power or source of inspiration is, we share the value of faith.

The second core value is relationships with loved ones. This may include strengthening the bonds we have with family, friends, coworkers, and maybe even pets. Most of us have at least one relationship we cherish, but if you don't, my guess is that you long for one. Belonging is a fundamental need, and we place a high value on these human bonds. Love is at the core of every successful relationship, and we all have a need to love and be loved. Relationships give us purpose and help foster personal growth.

Most of us want to progress in this life. Whether or not we are currently doing anything about it, we recognize the need to learn and improve ourselves, and desire a better life. The third core value is personal development, and it has many facets. Some of us may want to be more punctual, better organized, or a harder worker. We may also want to develop a more positive attitude, improve our financial security, or pursue a personal passion. Regardless what we are seeking to develop, every one of us wants to improve ourselves in some way.

The fourth core value is health. No matter where we live in this world, all human beings should care about their health. Being healthy gives us a greater quality of life and increased longevity. Being healthy allows us more enjoyment with those we love, doing the things we love. Being aware of our bodies' needs by eating healthy and being physically fit will actually save us money in the long run and keep us from experiencing possible setbacks from poor health.

The last core value is personal resources, particularly time and money. Whether we are wealthy or living in poverty, we all value financial resourcefulness and those freedoms that come as a result. Oftentimes it is not the material objects that we wish to possess, but the peace of mind and time to pursue what we desire in life. Time allows us quality experiences with loved ones, precious moments reserved for exercise and meditation, and learning opportunities to reach our goals.

As we establish goals, it is vital that we focus our time and energy on these five core values in order to reaffirm our faith, seek quality relationships, develop our talents and personal attributes, take care of our bodies, and practice good management of our time and money. If we neglect any one of these five areas, we will eventually cripple our progress in life and find ourselves off balance, unhappy, and dissatisfied with life. The only way to achieve total balance and total success is by centering our goals on our core values, and aligning ourselves with the benefits and results we hope to gain. Rest assured that when you begin to understand how to apply the seven formulas to the five core values of your life, there will be no stopping you!

Make It Count

Every thought, word, and action in our lives contributes to our success in each of our five core values and our overall potential.

Those seemingly meaningless words we utter really do make a difference in our attitude and our dedication to accomplishing our goals. Those day-to-day thoughts and actions add up, and pretty soon our lives are over and we ask ourselves, "What have I really accomplished?" Oftentimes we have regrets and wish we would have done more with our lives, and we repeat the words, "If I had to do it over again, I would've . . ."

Our goal should be to make the most of every day so that we lead a full, meaningful life, free of regrets. Now, this may sound wonderful but far reaching, especially when piles of laundry are heaping up, screaming kids are demanding our attention, bills need to get paid, and life events weigh us down. While we will have days that are tough and thoughts of despair cross our minds, there is hope if we will persist and not settle for a mediocre life. We must believe that our existence was meant to be happy and that no matter what life throws our way, we can make the best of our circumstances and rise above the chaos to achieve a life of happiness and fulfillment. If we cling to that hope, we will focus on what we really want, be relentless in our determination to succeed, and rise above the trials of life.

When we were kids we were told that we could become anything we set our minds to, and we believed it wholeheartedly. We would use our imaginations to create limitless futures of what we could do with our potential. Then as we got older, we grew doubtful and let people tell us who we were or what our worth was. Maybe as a result we've begun to grow calloused and sometimes bitter, and eventually have given up on the dreams we fascinated about as kids. To all of you who have given up on those dreams and have decided to lull yourself into a life of mediocrity and complacency, I say,

"Please snap out of it and take your life back." When you're telling your kids that they can become whatever they set their minds to, and they look up at you and say, "Mommy, are you living your dreams?" how will you feel and what will you say?

Every one of us is unique and has certain talents and capabilities that make us who we are. We also have unlimited ability and resources in maximizing our potential in life. We can do amazing things and tap into a reservoir of potential. The first step in accessing this power is expanding our vision of what is possible.

Dream without Limits

Look around and see the amazing accomplishments of humankind. We have sent a man to the moon, discovered how to create an airplane and an automobile, found cures for certain forms of cancer, and created incredible skyscrapers that fill our cities. All of these miracles we once thought to be impossible have now happened. Now, you may be telling yourself, "Those amazing discoveries were made by really smart people, but I can't do those things." Don't you see that your view of yourself is what limits who you are? If those men and women responsible for such genius in this world thought they could never do it, they wouldn't have. They believed that they could do anything, and therefore they did it.

Dreaming big means realizing that you have an unlimited amount of potential in life and that you can achieve anything you set your mind to. My mother was an awesome teacher of this principle. When I was a boy, she would hold me and tell me that I could do anything. She filled my mind with a perception that I could be the best at whatever I did. Her words were the initial seeds of a relentless determination to reach my potential and make my dreams a reality. I've seen this same effect in each of my siblings, and I give great credit to my mother for teaching me this principle when I was at a very early age. My mother raised us kids to expect the very best of ourselves—nothing less—and I will always be thankful to her for instilling this principle in my life.

Now some may say, "I didn't have a mother to teach me that, in fact, my parents or siblings were negative and didn't teach me properly." If this is the case, then what a great opportunity to change and to start a legacy in your own life of recognizing your potential and passing this on to your posterity. Master this trait and let it become a guiding force for you and those around you.

We all experience this life, but it's what we do with it that makes it extraordinary. To do so we must thrive and not just survive. We can rise to amazing heights when we push back the barriers of our own limiting beliefs and stretch our thoughts to what we can become. How big can you dream? Can you get past yourself to see who you can become? Can you get out of your own way and let yourself evolve into greatness?

Years ago I saw an advertisement by Nike that stressed this same principle of following through on our dreams. The spokesperson for this ad was Barry Sanders, the great running back for the Detroit Lions who displayed exceptional drive in following his dreams. Despite his phenomenal years of football in both the NCAA and the NFL, setting countless records, receiving the Heisman Trophy, and being named MVP, in high school Sanders didn't earn a starting position on the football team until his senior year and then again in college until his junior year. Sander's actions clearly reflect the patience and persistence that accompany true success and remind us to not let anything stand in the way of our dreams. The only way to overcome fear and meet success head on is to "just do it," as this Nike advertisement reads.

Too often we are scared. Scared of what we might not be able to do. Scared of what people might think if we tried. We let our fears stand in the way of our hopes. We say no when we want to say yes. We sit quietly when we want to scream. And we shout with the others when we should keep our mouths shut. Why? After all, we do only go around once. There's really no time to be afraid. So stop. Try something you've never tried. Risk it. Enter a triathlon. Write a letter to the editor. Demand a raise. Call winners at the toughest court. Throw away your television. Bicycle across the United States. Try bobsledding. Try anything. Speak out against the designated hitter. Travel to a country where you don't speak the language. Patent something. Call her. You have nothing to lose and everything, everything, everything to gain. JUST DO IT.

Expanding your vision means throwing by the wayside thoughts of what you can't do and concentrating on all the things you can do. We must change our focus in order to foster a new frame of mind that is conducive to reaching our potential and realizing our dreams. If you want a more effective and fulfilling life, change is imperative. The good news is that you absolutely can do it.

As If Principle

Past senior officer at Citibank and CEO of Grindlay's Bank, Wilford Farnsworth taught me a valuable principle when I was a young man. It is called the *As If Principle*, and it changed my life forever. The idea of the As If Principle originally came from William James, considered by many to be the father of psychology. James said that if you want a certain quality, act "as if" you already had it. For the As If Principle to truly work to your advantage, your desires must be based on correct principles. My good friend Farnsworth prefaced his explanation as such to prevent anyone from effortlessly applying the As If Principle for false treasure without a willingness to work for it. The As If Principle says that if you want something in life, write it down "as if" you've achieved it, and you will receive it. Sounds easy and a little hokey right? That's what I thought too until I applied it and began to see amazing results in my life. The explanation of this, however, will make more sense.

The As If Principle works and can be applied to every facet of life. First create a list of positive affirmations of anything you would like to achieve and review this list daily, repeating aloud and focusing on these accomplishments "as if" you had done them. Do this for thirty days and see the difference. You will begin to embody the list of positive affirmations you created, and your life will change for the better. When applied correctly, the As If Principle can expand our capacities and will allow us to tap into a reservoir of unlimited potential that will maximize all we do.

When you write something down and say it, your mind doesn't filter what it is being told and therefore believes what you say. As your mind processes that information over time, your actions and words begin to mirror that input. Let me give you an example. If you wanted to be more efficient at work, and you knew that being focused and hardworking are based on moral principles, you would write down, "I am an effective worker and remain focused on the task before me." You would then feed that into your brain by saying it consistently over time. Your mind would then begin to believe what you had told it, and in time your behavior would reflect this result. I call this *cognitive transformation*—the act of applying a positive stimulus to one's very thought processes and thus converting them into the desired action and objective.

When I create positive affirmations, I consider the five core values of faith, relationships, personal development, health, and resources (time and money). These universal values encapsulate what we as human beings care most about in life, so by focusing on these five core areas, we are better able to identify our true goals and create the most effective positive affirmations. List as many statements about one value as you would like. Then repeat this same process for each of the five core values, creating a list of positive affirmations that you can repeat every day.

For the core value of faith, you might say, "I know that I'm capable of anything I put my mind to," "I trust God and know that He can help me overcome any challenge," or "I tap into my limitless potential by obeying natural laws." For relationships maybe you would write, "I spend quality time with my family and friends," "I show appreciation to others," or "I look for the best in the people around me." And for personal development you might say, "I have a positive attitude," "I give 100 percent in everything I do," and "I choose my thoughts, actions, and words with wisdom." You are not limited to the five core values, but most, if not all, of your positive affirmations will fall into one of these five areas. These statements are just for you, so don't be bashful—let your imagination and pen run wild with those things you want to be.

The As If Principle will work with anything we do as long as we base it on correct principles. We can't say, "I want a million dollars," and then do nothing of our own volition to obtain this, or say, "I am in fantastic shape," but then sit on the couch all day eating Twinkies and chips—we cannot fool the formula for success. Now, we could also apply these cognitive transformations to prosperity or health if we were to back them with a plan of action—words alone will not produce the result.

The idea behind the As If Principle is not some trivial "just say I can do anything in the mirror a hundred times and I can do it" type of principle. Rather, the As If Principle allows people to move past their own limiting beliefs and put their attention on what they can do. These positive affirmations, when repeated over a thirty-day span, will become engrained in you. When you form a daily habit of repeating these affirmations "as if" you are that type of person, your actions will begin to validate them. This really works and will seem almost magical; yet, these effective and successful results are an actual physiological change that produces actions to match our thoughts. As we focus on our desires and abilities, the body and mind respond and seek to validate our words. We are more driven to action because we are focused on the results we are looking for. In fact, the results are only manifested as we complement the thought with the action. Once again, timeless principles follow a law that when obeyed yield a result.

Many of today's scientific studies support the idea that positive thinking not only provides us with a more satisfying life but also plays a key role in our physical health. In support of the As If Principle, in November 2004 an article titled "Dispositional Optimism and All-Cause and Cardiovascular Mortality in a Prospective Cohort of Elderly Dutch Men and Women" was published in *Archives of General Psychiatry*. Over a nine-year period this study examined 941 Dutch men and women between the ages of sixty-five and eighty-five. After determining the subjects' levels of optimism or pessimism, researchers looked at the death rate of these individuals some ten years later. Subjects with the most optimistic attitude had a death rate of 30.4 percent versus a death rate of 56.5 percent among the subjects with the most pessimistic attitude. In addition to this study, a 2003 report from the National Alliance on Mental Illness stated that cognitive based therapies (CBTs), which are therapies to help change one's thinking pattern and thereby change the way one feels, have shown to effectively treat depression, anxiety disorders, and eating disorders. Countless other scientific studies support the idea that positive thinking adds value to our lives and contributes to our overall physical health, giving us all the more reason to implement the As If Principle in our daily lives.

The As If Principle is used by top performing athletes, CEOs of companies, and moms all over the world. This principle has been responsible for taking people to new levels of performance and has allowed them to reach unimaginable heights. When we decide what we want out of life, write down our goals, and speak of our dreams "as if" we've achieved them, everything we do will collaborate to their realization.

Be Productive

All human beings have the ability to be productive with their time and opportunities, and reach their unlimited potential. It makes no difference if you are white, black, brown, or green. It makes no difference if you are male or female. No one gets a free ride to a balanced life and total success in all five core values—there is no shortcut, there is no way around hard work. We all possess unique talents, interests, and passions, and are characterized by different temperaments and personalities, but we do share the traits of having a mind, body, and spirit. It's what we do with that mind, body, and spirit that make us different.

How do you spend your time? Do you dwell on useless matters or on things of value? Rather than senselessly wasting time on differences of skin color or whether men are more dominant than women or visa versa, it would be more beneficial to devote our time to productive matters that actually make a difference in the world. We are much better off nurturing and developing our mind, body, and spirit in a positive and magnificent way instead of creating negative energy that has no purpose and gains us nothing.

I am married to the most wonderful woman in the world. She has to put up with my positive mumbo jumbo all the time. My wife knows that I try to spend very little energy on negativity, whether it be talking badly of others or dealing with a dead-end problem. I try to spend my time on things I can do, not on things out of my control. Some may say that being constantly positive is unrealistic, but I say that reality is what you make it. We are given twenty-four hours in a day, and we have the choice to either waste that precious time on negativity or to be productive and spend our time and energy on the positives of this world. I'm not saying that tough things won't happen, because they will, but I am saying that we can make the most of every situation. Spending days focused in a positive manner will improve our quality of life, help us be our best at all times, and attract people to us.

Positive Surround Sound

Surround yourself—your mind, body, and spirit—with the best stuff. Surround yourself with positive music, people, books, quotes, stories, art, and anything that will motivate you to be all you can be. Why not? We have the ability to choose these influences. Have you ever noticed how wonderful it is to be around someone who talks about the positive side of life and its goodness and all the things you can do, rather than people who occupy their time with all the doom and gloom in the world? Be someone who lifts people to be their best and not one who sucks the life out of everyone.

Some may say that dwelling on the positive is easy when you don't have any problems. I think this is a total excuse. I find it interesting when people think that individuals with a positive nature are that way as a result of an easy life; oftentimes it's just the opposite. We often have no idea what tremendous challenges those positive-minded individuals have faced or are facing. Although I prefer to focus on the positive, I too fall prey to negativity at times and many other errors in life, from which I have tried to learn. However, with all those things said, I would rather focus the majority of my time bettering my life and the lives of others than the alternative.

On a scale from one to ten, where are you with your faith, relationships, personal development, health, and resources of time and money? Ask yourself what is stopping you from being at a ten in each area. Try to identify what is standing in your way of success. You may find that your roadblock is self-doubt or fear. Or maybe the friends you surround yourself with are not good influences and don't inspire you to reach your dreams. A real friend should make you want to be your best and do things that would help create an encouraging environment. We should strive to be a positive influence for everyone around us.

As you take a personal inventory of each aspect of your life, you will begin to identify those influences that are impeding your progress and keeping you from being at a ten. Your roadblock in health may be those late-night munchies or your inability to exercise. Maybe having snacks in the house is too tempting, and you should keep them out of the cupboards until the weekend. Surround yourself with influences that will stack the odds in your favor for success.

As we take a personal inventory of our lives and become more aware of those roadblocks keeping us from our dreams, we will be able to make the necessary changes to ensure our success. Choose to surround yourself with positive influences that motivate and inspire you to greatness. I promise you that eliminating the negativity and distractions will keep you focused and give you greater motivation to reach your true potential.

Attitude Is Everything

The world we create around us is a product of how we view it. Our every thought, word, and action contributes to our attitude and thus our overall potential, either bolstering it or deflating it. Those seemingly meaningless words we utter, either laced with negativity or exuding positivity, really do make a difference. When you look at others, do you see their flaws or their strengths? How do you see yourself? To see the potential around us, we must look for the best in others and in ourselves. Often we get so caught up with our own doubts and fears that we have a hard time seeing outside our own tainted lenses of life and therefore hold ourselves back from our true potential. To be our best we must think about what we can do and not about what we can't.

I have some very good friends who find the best in life and in the people they are around. Life seems so refreshing and positive when I am with them—I love it. They have their share of struggles, yet they are able to find the value in what they are going through and use it for their good. They are the kind of people who add to life and make everything seem better. We should seek out these types of friends and be this kind of friend for others. Life is what you make of it, so why not make it positive?

Our attitude defines who we are. Two people facing the same illness may have strikingly different perspectives on the ordeal. One may talk about everything they can't do and how miserable it is to be bedridden, while the other individual may choose to dwell on the things they can do and take a completely different approach to their sickness. The positive-minded individual may see the illness as a chance to redirect his or her focus in life and show greater appreciation for the aspects of good health he or she still has. The point is that it is not our circumstances in life that define us, but rather it is the attitude we maintain through those circumstances. We can't control what happens to us, but we can control how we react.

Many recent scientific studies have shown how positive thinking has an undeniable affect on our physical and mental health. *The New York Times* reported that researchers at the University of Wisconsin found evidence linking positive emotions with a stronger immune response when people receive a flu vaccine. The anticipation of a medicine, or vaccine in this case, literally causes the human body to release endorphins to aid in that medicine. The United States–based Mayo Clinic, an internationally known nonprofit group, presented additional research in their article "Positive Thinking: Reduce Stress and Enjoy Life More," saying that positive thinking is a "stress management skill" associated with a number of positive benefits, including greater resistance to the common cold, decreased negative stress, lower rates of depression, better coping skills during difficult times, and better psychological and physical well-being. The state of our attitude has everything to do with the health of our bodies, and therefore the success we experience in life.

Now that we know how influential our attitudes are, we can focus on improving them as we look for the good all around us. Surround yourself with people, media, and other influences that will motivate you and bring out the best in you. I have a positive room in my home where I surround myself with those things that matter most to me. Uplifting art hangs on the walls, along with motivating quotes, beautiful pictures of my family, and memorabilia of achievements in my life. Other items that represent and contribute to my values and passions in life are also found there. This room has become an escape for me, where I can seek wisdom and inspiration while surrounded by motivating influences for good. Wherever your sanctuary of peace and solace may be, go there for strength and for a fresh and positive perspective on life.

We find in life exactly what we are looking for, good or bad. If we look for faults in others, we will find all those things that annoy us; however, if we look for the strengths of an individual, that is what we will see. We get exactly what we are looking for. Have you ever shopped for a new or used car, found a make and model you liked, and then suddenly noticed that particular kind of car everywhere you went? And before then you'd never even known that car existed. The same principle applies in all aspects of life; we will see what we are looking for. Find the best in everything around you, and your life will be full of passion and peace. When we look to find fault with the world and with others, our perspective takes a negative turn. There is so much good to be found if we are looking for it.

Test of Life

This experience of life is like an enormous test. How will we do? Will we pass? How will we be remembered after we die? What will others say of who you were and what kind of life you represented? I would imagine that each of us would choose to be remembered as someone who always gave 100 percent, someone who took time for others, someone who had the right priorities and lived by correct principles. You can live this life and you can start today, right now this very instant. Once this day passes you by, you will never get it over again, so be productive and let today take you one step closer to accomplishing your dreams.

Our test of life is to see if we can prioritize our values and achieve excellence in the areas that matter the most. Because we all share the five core values, we have the opportunity to bond together in our quest of excellence as we live this life. As we determine those values that should guide our lives and then live true to those principles that we know to be right, we will establish a sense of peace, happiness, and balance in our lives. When and only when we live by correct principles, we will begin to prosper and grow. So think of the big picture and what you ultimately want out of your life. Determine your values and then write them down, being aware of your highest priorities. Without a plan we are left to wander and waste precious time.

Clear your mind for a minute, and without any preconceived notions, fears, or hesitations, identify those areas of your life that matter most to you. What brings you the most satisfaction? If you had all the time in the world, where would you spend that time? Would it be with family, in the pursuit of a certain passion like traveling or fly-fishing, or strengthening your faith? Most people spend their free time doing what matters most to them, so decide now where you will invest your time and how you will create value in this world.

I remember attending the funeral for an extended family member. This man was the source of strength and inspiration to many, as evidenced by the sweet comments countless individuals shared. I reflected on the tremendous influence that one person had on so many others. This man had taken time for those things that mattered most. People were not concerned with his career, the car he drove, how much money he made, or any other trivial matter. Instead people remembered him for how he had touched their lives. This experience had a great impact on me, and afterward I committed to live my life in a more meaningful way.

Part of passing the test of life is reaching our highest potential. Why would we want anything less for ourselves? We all have it in us to be our very best, so in reality we don't need to compare ourselves to others. We are uniquely designed with varying talents and abilities. Don't worry if Jane plays the piano beautifully and you can't even plunk out Chopsticks, or that Bob was high school high jump champ and you and your lead feet seldom cleared the bar, or that Nancy seems to manage all eight of her children with ease and you are overwhelmed with two. Be grateful to be you. How boring would this life be if we all were masters at the same things? We tend to compare our worst with another person's best and that just isn't fair to ourselves. You can do things that no one else can do, so take the time to identify and then focus on those unique gifts so that you don't lose them from neglect. You are in charge and you can choose, so choose today to be the best you.

Realizing who we are and what we are capable of takes work. We can't expect to gain extraordinary results with ordinary thinking. Our human capacity to reach our potential is like a muscle. When we exercise it, we can gain great strength. When it goes unused, it withers and begins to atrophy. Every day we must realize that we can and will reach our potential—that we can be our best at all times, in all places, under any circumstances. We must dream big to break through those barriers that hold us back. We must fill our minds with positive uplifting thoughts and change our current way of thinking. We must surround ourselves with positive influences to stimulate and enhance our perception of life and ourselves.

Sometimes during this test of life we let obstacles slow us down. We allow people to thwart our dreams. We let others decide who we are and what will become of us, impeding our plans and curtailing our potential. If you are under this influence, stop right now and realize that you can become anything you desire and that you are not a by-product of someone else's jealousy, criticism, fear, envy, or whatever tainted lens they are looking through. When people are miserable they like to bring others down with them. If we play into this scene, our potential will always be a fleeting thought. But your potential is not fleeting—it is sure and comes from within you. Never forget that. This test we're living is to continually overcome the obstacles we're faced with and to continue moving forward. All of us will trip at times, but as we continue to get up and move forward, we will get closer and closer to realizing the ultimate potential within us.

I grew up with some great young men in high school, but they quickly fell prey to partying and mischievousness. One of them was a good friend of mine and, after a while, wanted to change his life and get away from those destructive forces. He would drink at the parties, and his peers would egg him on so that gradually everyone expected reckless behavior from him. When this young man decided to change his life, he got heckled and told, "Who're you kidding? You're a partier and always will be." Instead of believing in himself and holding to correct principles, this young man buckled and fell back into this pit of destructive pressure. I wondered for a time what became of him, what he did with his life. I wondered what he may have become if he had dreamed big and believed in himself. I felt bad for him then but even more so when I learned that his life had not amounted to much and that some of his influenced behavior had led him into an adult life of addiction. The test of life had beaten him down and kept him down; whereas, if he'd stayed strong in his initial decision to change, he may have gotten up.

Will you pass the test of life? How you fair is primarily determined by you. Don't let others tell you who you are or what you'll become. Decide now that you will pass the test well. Your thoughts and attitudes will contribute to your grade, and you will accomplish what you think you can. If you don't believe it, just look around you and dissect your own life to see whether or not your thoughts have been indicative of your results. Your grade is not based on how many times you fell but how many times you got back up. The determination to get back up is what makes the difference and what determines one's success.

Recap: Results

This first formula states that within each of us is unlimited potential and that the only limitations in life are those we place upon ourselves. We must dream big and realize our full capacity in life. To do this we must change our way of thinking and surround ourselves with positive influences, letting these influences stimulate our thoughts and drive us to realize our dreams.

If you will master the Seven Formulas of Success, starting with this first one, you will accomplish whatever dream your mind can conceive. Break the shackles that limit you and rip through the barriers that hold you back. Dream big—your potential is limitless and your success is just a thought away.

Formula 2:
Power to Choose

Success is not a matter of chance but a matter of choice.

You Have the Power

As we come to more fully understand our true potential, we naturally are better able to make decisions and choose what will lead us toward our goals. Ultimately we are responsible for the outcome of our lives. Some of you may be thrilled by this news, while others of you may want to crawl in a hole or slam this book shut because you're tired of hearing that you're supposedly in control of your life when that's the last thing you feel. If responsibility makes you run or you struggle to make decisions or you don't feel like you can rise above the life you are enduring, please keep reading.

Senior pastor Charles Swindoll has written more than thirty best-selling books on how to improve our lives and take responsibility for our circumstances. Often when I think about the power we possess to make our lives what we choose, I think of Swindoll's poem "Attitude":

The longer I live, the more I realize the impact of attitude on life.

Attitude, to me, is more important than facts. It is more important than the past, than education, than money, than circumstances, than failures, than successes, than what other people think or say or do. It is more important than appearance, giftedness, or skill. It will make or break a company . . . a church . . . a home.

The remarkable thing is we have a choice every day regarding the attitude we will embrace for that day. We cannot change our past . . . we cannot change the fact that people will act in a certain way. We cannot change the inevitable. The only thing we can do is play on the one string we have, and that is our attitude. . . . I am convinced that life is 10 percent what happens to me and 90 percent how I react to it.

And so it is with you . . . we are in charge of our attitudes.

Regardless what you may think right now, believe me when I say that you do possess unlimited potential, and you determine your attitude and ultimately your destiny. "Success is not a matter of chance but a matter of choice," as Formula 2 states, and no one can take that from you unless you let them. Starting this very moment, you decide how the chapters of your life will unfold and how your story will end. I didn't say that the story would be without struggle—we can't always control the events that transpire—but we always hold the power to choose how we will react. You have the power to choose every day, and your life will ultimately be a culmination of these choices.

Choose Success

Success is not an outcome that sneaks up on us one morning and waits patiently at the foot of our bed until we wake up. We literally must choose success and call it ours and keep telling ourselves it's ours on numerous occasions of any given day. You may not realize it, but as you are reading this page you are making choices. Even as we speak, you are choosing the very thoughts that come into your mind. Try to dissect them and identify their nature. Most of us go through life not realizing that we are making choices in every moment and that those choices will determine the success of our lives. Become aware of the opportunities before you every moment. Now this may sound somewhat exhausting, but in the end you will see fantastic results come into your life as you apply this second formula for success. Learning to recognize that we have a choice is the first step in mastering this formula.

Most of us have approximately sixty thousand thoughts race through our minds in a given day. Do we take responsibility for those thoughts? Do we have a desire to control such thoughts? The second step in mastering Formula 2 and achieving success is understanding that our choices have consequences, good or bad, and that ultimately our choices determine our success or failure in life. To gain results in life and achieve your dreams, you must check into the game and know that you get to call the shots—you choose what happens because it's your life. Checking into the game means you are not content just watching others succeed in the game of life. You want to participate, you want to contribute, you want to win! You can complain, blame others, or make excuses, but you are responsible for where you take your thoughts. Now I am not saying that we'll never have occasional thoughts that are out of line with our values, but what we do with those thoughts is our responsibility.

Let me give you an example. Imagine you are trying to lose weight and get in better shape, so you start an exercise program. Some weeks down the road, or maybe even during those initial days of working out, your mind may register the thought, "I don't think I can do it." You basically have two choices of what to do with that thought: you can let that idea discourage you to the point that you give up completely and go eat a pint of Ben & Jerry's, or you can decide that even though you don't want to keep working out, it's good for you and it's what you must do to gain what you ultimately want. If we take charge, we can channel our scattered thoughts that contradict our goals and make them work for us instead of against us. Positive thoughts can help us gain an even clearer view of our values and remember that we have the power to choose and we're choosing to succeed. Try starting the day by saying, "I am in charge, and I decide what I will become." It may sound corny, but it's true.

The third step to making success a matter of choice is taking responsibility for our decisions by taking action toward our desired goals. Being responsible for our choices is liberating. When we begin to see that we determine the course of our lives, the whole world will open up to us, and we'll see with new eyes that there's nothing we can't accomplish—nothing will hold us back from the life we want.

My family and I like to sit down together and watch NBC's television program *The Biggest Loser*. The interesting thing is that this show teaches the contestants that they're responsible for their choices, the very same principle Formula 2 confirms. The participants want so desperately to improve their health and well-being, and when they finally realize that they have a choice in the matter and that their poor health condition is a result of their neglect and bad choices, you can see a light go on in their heads. The competitors suddenly realize that they've been blaming their overweight condition on supposed uncontrollable factors. They quickly realize that they are in charge and have the power to fix the mess they made of their bodies. I love seeing their growth and this formula in action. The moment they grasp this principle, you can see their determination to make up for lost time in their lives and take on the world.

This formula, "Success is not a matter of chance but a matter of choice," can be applied in every aspect of our lives, not just health. It works in our occupations, how we treat our families, and how we pursue our lifelong dreams. Let's take an example of how this principle can apply in our jobs. I worked as a financial advisor for many years. I really enjoyed working with others and helping them to achieve their financial and personal dreams. As a rookie stockbroker, I was eager to come off to a great start. I studied hard for my series seven, a qualification required to trade securities (stocks, bonds, etc.) on behalf of another, and the many other licenses required to manage the portfolios of my clients. I wanted to be well prepared to manage their assets in the best possible manner. Since I began with a top firm, I was able to come out of the gate with some great success and eventually was recognized as one of the top performing rookie stockbrokers in the country. I worked extremely hard and had a genuine interest in my clients' success.

During this time, other stockbrokers in the office started wondering what I was doing to find new clients. I had fellow brokers approach me and ask me what my secret was. I informed them that there really was no big secret except for making good use of time. There was no magic pill or lucky rabbit's foot—just good old-fashioned work and taking responsibility for my time. It seemed the harder I worked, the luckier I got.

Many of the brokers in my office would often goof off during the workday. They would play putt-putt golf down the hall and constantly take long lunches, leaving to do eighteen holes, and then wonder why they were not getting results from their efforts. One day I took aside another rookie broker who was seeking advice. He was struggling and wanted some tips on finding new clients. I said, "I will tell you how to be successful in this business, and it will work if you do exactly what I say." He perked up and said he would follow my instructions to the tee. I said, "Sit in this chair and for six months make cold calls eight hours a day. If you do this, you will never have to cold call again in this business, and you will have constant referrals going forward. Your clientele will grow, and you will acquire new assets to manage." He vowed to follow this very simple advice, however a week later I saw him fall into the same lazy practices he had before. He left the business after one year.

The point of this story is that we have the power to choose our destiny, but we must be willing to pay the price for success. We must take responsibility for our choices, because these choices will influence our success in all that we do. I was a decent stockbroker, but my real success came from learning this formula and taking responsibility for my choices. We cannot change the law; we can kick against it and try to fight it, but the law will ultimately bestow its reward.

Make the Reason Worth the Price

When we face decisions on a daily basis, it is easy to get sucked into the black hole of excuses and neglect our opportunity to choose success. Our decisions become based on "the pain and pleasure" principle, meaning that we as human beings tend to gravitate to the area that causes the least amount of pain. While this may look appealing on the outside, a deeper sense of purpose on the inside is ready to emerge. The key is to identify the real reason why you are pursuing your goal and to make the reason worth the price for the reward.

Let's again take the example of losing weight. Losing weight may initially sound fairly painful because we know that to accomplish this goal it would require some physical exertion and the sacrifice of our favorite treats. Therefore we associate more pleasure with not working out and enjoying food without discretion. This rationale appears convincing on the outside, and we may even talk ourselves into believing this falsehood; however, if we look closer within ourselves, we will discover that ultimately there is more pleasure and freedom in being fit. Despite the sacrifices required to obtain it, we recognize that the true pain is being overweight and the challenges that poor health presents. Once we get past the initial analysis, we see that preserving and maintaining our health will ultimately produce much more pleasure than staying out of shape ever could. Health is worth the price. So next time you are waffling on your plan of action to accomplish your goal, remind yourself of your greater reason to pay the price for success.

Step four in choosing success is committing to a lifetime of choices that turn your dreams into reality. What are your dreams? Can you deal with the pain of not achieving those dreams? Is your dream to be financially independent? If so, what would be the consequences of not achieving that dream? Not being able to do the things you love to do, not having financial peace of mind, or maybe even not being able to pay your bills? When you uncover the pain and sacrifice that goes along with realizing your dreams, you will come to the conclusion that there is greater pain in not reaching that goal. Write down any area you desire to change in your life. Then write down the pain of not accomplishing that goal. If a dream is of real value, there will be much greater pleasure in attaining that dream than there is pain and consequence in its absence.

Mental Scripts

As we pursue lives of excellence, we face both internal and external challenges with the decisions we make. We form mental scripts, both positive and negative, based on the way we view the world and hear other scripts that originate from how others view the world. Some of these perspectives can be very energizing and others can suck the life out of you. Surround yourself with good energy and try to be a positive influence on those around you who are also struggling—we are responsible for feeding mental scripts to others too.

You do not have to buy into any mind-set or opinion that you don't agree with, so don't waste your time or energy with thoughts that will inhibit and diminish your full potential. It's your job to choose, so choose wisely. If we choose, mental scripts can enliven our thoughts and create a mentality of potential and opportunity.

I choose to dwell on mental scripts that allow me to be my best and make the best of where I am at that given time. Now, some may say that it's not realistic to always think optimistically because sometimes bad things just happen. I agree that life can deal us some challenges at times; however, to me reality is making the best of whatever your conditions may be. Life may throw us some curve balls at times, but we can choose how we react.

I went to a large real estate convention in Las Vegas several years ago. One of the keynote speakers was the wife of Christopher Reeves, the famous actor from the motion picture *Superman*, whose character we all came to know and love. In 1995 Reeves was in a tragic horse riding incident, which left him paralyzed from the neck down. His wife talked about the tough challenges that accompanied this horrific condition. She related how tough this was for her husband and that there were many dark days and tiring nights as he tried to adjust to his new physical condition. Some would've thrown in the towel at this point and checked out of life, feeling they were justified given the circumstances. But Reeves did not choose this option for himself. Instead he made the very best of his circumstances and became a real-life hero due to how he responded to this challenge. He became an inspiration to his wife and to the world because of the positive attitude he embraced. He made the very best of his circumstances and became a real-life "super man."

I love to hear stories of everyday men and women who, in the face of adversity, rise to the occasion and become heroes to us all. Most of these heroes aren't famous but are the mothers and fathers who, despite their financial challenges, go to work and find a way to support their families and sacrifice for those they love. Some of these everyday heroes are those who, despite grave danger to them, fight for their country in order to preserve the freedoms we enjoy each day. Some of these heroes are those who fight the battles of cancer or diabetes, struggle for life while keeping their chin up, and motivate those around them. Our reality in life is making the very best of our everyday circumstances and rising above our challenges to gain victory for ourselves and for those around us.

We choose our mental scripts every day no matter what life sends our way. Take time to condition yourself to create positive mental scripts and seek to motivate others to do the same. We're all in this together and can inspire each other along the way to achieving our life goals. These mental scripts help shape our efforts and empower us to realize our dreams. Create positive mental scripts within yourself by choosing to focus on what you can do. We can unlock the power of success if we will apply this formula to our lives, remembering that success is not a matter of chance—we choose to make it happen.

Focus on What You Want

As we embrace our newfound freedom of choice, we can use this power to tackle our goals and realize our dreams. This power comes from focusing on what we want, not on what we don't want. When you identify your values, you must focus entirely on the result that you wish to gain. Some dwell on the antithesis of this model, for example, focusing on how little time they have instead of maximizing their time. People who want to be financially self-sufficient dwell on all the money they can save instead of on all the items they can't buy. The difference between these two perspectives is that the mind gravitates to what we dwell on, thus diverting our attention either toward or away from the goal. If we choose to focus on what we wish to accomplish, this very act of visualization will propel us toward claiming the prize.

Visualization is when we focus on what we want and picture ourselves attaining it. A person who applies this tool strengthens his or her chances of acquiring the desired result because attaining the goal becomes routine. You get to the point where you think, "Well, of course I'm going to do it. I've already done it fifteen times in my mind, so it's second nature now." Athletes utilize this tool for accomplishing great results in their performance. By visualizing the act of attaining your goal, you prepare yourself for success and expect success. This mental process activates emotions similar to the actual result and triggers a physical and emotional response of action. A basketball player who visualizes himself at the free throw line, making basket after basket, actually puts himself in an emotional state of mind that focuses on the intended result. This powerful state of mind triggers an emotional and physical sense of being in that moment, performing this action. When people are able to visualize accomplishing their goals, they often can't tell much difference between the simulated and the actual. They feel that they have been there before and have practiced it hundreds of times.

Choosing to focus specifically on what you want can contribute to your success in a powerful way. Take a moment to visualize your dreams and those results you are looking for in every aspect of your life. What kind of husband or wife, father or mother do you see yourself being? How would you prefer to raise and treat your children? What kind of friend do you hope to be? What hobbies or talents do you envision yourself developing? What type of financial condition would you like to find yourself in? Choose positive thoughts for attaining the results you desire. Then write these goals down, focusing on what you want. Read them daily and solidify them in your mind so that they become part of who you are. Make a copy of these goals and carry them with you in your planner, keep them in your car, or post them on your bedroom mirror. Put them in a place where they are easily accessible. This power to visualize will play a key role in your success and can powerfully influence your future quality of life.

Recap: Sacrifice Brings Rewards

The power to choose is yours. It's offered at no monetary cost, but it does require sacrifice and a new perspective. Learning to exercise this power is just like starting to work out a muscle: it doesn't happen overnight, but the more you practice making good decisions, the easier it will get and the stronger you will become. As you exercise the power to choose, your strength to make wise decisions will increase, and you'll be on course to pursue and accomplish your dreams.

Part of exercising this power to choose is being willing to sacrifice old habits and inconsistent patterns that don't work. Be willing to let go of your old thought processes and discover a new and powerful model of success. You can practice this every day, even if you begin to change only a few thoughts as you go. Baby steps lead to big steps, and big steps lead to big dreams, so keep moving.

Once you've mastered the ability to choose your response, your thoughts will unlock endless possibilities, and you'll see your words and actions fall in line. Your thoughts become those words that leave your lips as well as the actions you perform. Since we are a makeup of these components, most people gain a perspective of who you are based on your thoughts, words, and actions. You may have already seen how the power to choose is directly linked to these three areas of interpretation and communication.

Those actions and words we exhibit were first created upon the scrolls of our minds. Therefore, by sacrificing and consciously striving to produce positive thoughts, we are able to produce positive actions and words. The rewards are there if we will take the time to master our choices. Sometimes this takes a lot of practice, but the effort will be worth the sacrifice. Some people spend a lifetime wondering why they can't get different results and yet are unwilling to sacrifice old habits. To get the reward and real success from life, we must be willing to do what it takes.

The power to choose is a freedom we all possess and is available this instant. Tap into it and become more aware of your ability to select how you will respond to life. Then use that agency to draw you closer to the life you want to live. As we take responsibility for our choices, we independently take charge of our destiny. The culmination of these choices will determine the life we lead and the legacy we leave behind. The power to choose is yours.

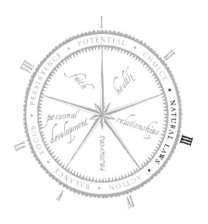

Formula 3:

Recipe for Success

Results stem from natural laws adhered to or broken.

The Law Is the Law

Just as science has established laws, life also has specific laws or formulas we must adhere to in order to achieve success. All things in the world follow laws—even the planets in our solar system obey the laws of space that keep them in orbit. If our earth did not follow the natural laws, we would be incinerated by the sun within seconds. These laws are what keep us safe and are the components from which we gain positive results. When we experience failure, we can usually trace it back to a natural law that we didn't follow.

Knowing the natural laws and obeying the formulas are what unlock success. Since we know that results stem from natural laws adhered to or broken, our goal is to follow the formulas and thereby reap inevitable success—the law is the law. Just as we will never be cheated by the system, we can never fool the system to get an equivalent result with a shortcut. A chef that skimps on a few key ingredients for a flavorful masterpiece will surely recognize the difference in taste and maybe even in appearance. Any time we deviate from the natural formulas and laws of success, we sacrifice the end result. When we take a shortcut or try to get the quick-fix result without paying the price of obedience to that natural law, we rob ourselves of freedom, power, and satisfaction.

In order to enjoy the fullness of life in all five of our core values we must learn the formulas for success and adhere to them so we can gain the desired result. We can literally become anything in life if we are willing to follow the formulas and pay the price. When we live in accordance with the natural laws and rules, we gain a reward; when we neglect these laws or try to take a shortcut, we reap a consequence. The old adage that we reap what we sow is a very true and very real principle.

Years ago I took a group of young men on a field trip to a county jail. The warden of the jail allowed this group of young men to visit with a few of the inmates. Those who were incarcerated in the jail were there for various reasons, including theft, substance abuse, and violence. They all shared one thing in common: they were suffering the consequences of breaking the law. This was an excellent experience for the boys as well as the adult leaders to recognize that our choices really do have consequences.

The young men had the opportunity to ask questions to the inmates. One question in particular that caught my attention was, "What decisions led you down this path of crime?" The commonly expressed answer was that each of these inmates had surrounded themselves with negative influences, ranging from bad music, to bad movies, to bad friends that served as catalysts that led them into crime. They concluded that their wrong choices had stolen their freedom, and now they were suffering the consequences. They noted that the illusion of wealth, sex, and getting high had lured them in and impaired their ability to make good choices. Their desire and actions for immediate gratification had led them into crimes that would imprison them for possibly the rest of their lives. This experience taught all of us a valuable lesson: laws are set up to keep us free, and when we obey those laws we have options. When we break those laws we lose the freedoms we once enjoyed as a consequence of our actions. Our ability to obey these laws is greatly influenced by the media and friends we surround ourselves with.

The World Is Your Classroom

One of the greatest blessings in life is the opportunity to learn. We can learn from everything that surrounds us. Sometimes we may feel like we need to be enrolled in school to gain an education or to learn the greatest things in life. This isn't necessarily true. I have learned more from my life experiences than anything I have ever learned in school. Now, don't get me wrong. I believe getting a formal education is important, but we must not miss out on the numerous opportunities to learn in our everyday lives. Every morning I wake up and think, "What can I learn today?" Can you imagine what knowledge you could gain by learning just one new idea per day?

If I were to tell you that the answers to life and success are found all around you, would that change the way you perceived your life? Would you spend more time learning if you knew that you could gain the treasures of knowledge on a daily basis if you just listened? By observing your surroundings daily, you can gain simple yet valuable wisdom and strengthen each of your core values, which include faith, relationships, personal development, health, and resources.

For example, I notice that when I serve others I feel happier—my own problems become swallowed up in my concern for the needs of others. I notice that when I eat poorly I have less energy and am less likely to want to engage in physical activity. I notice that when I pray I feel better and more optimistic about life. I notice that when I remember people's names they respond more favorably. We can gain simple yet observable treasures like these as we become more perceptive about our opportunities to learn. If we take the time to listen and learn from life, we can gain the wisdom to overcome any problem and achieve any dream.

My dad was a schoolteacher by profession and a masterful instructor at that. He always taught me that the best things in life are free, and I can't help but think that part of what he was referring to was the opportunity to learn on a daily basis. My dad finds such joy in living and experiencing life. At age eighty-two, he has a zest for life and still goes jogging in the cool of the morning. I often watch him, knowing his mind is contemplating the simple pleasures of life and what we can learn on a daily basis. After years of observing and learning from my father, I feel like I now share with him this enthusiasm for life and natural desire for knowledge.

Make this quest for learning a lifelong commitment. This opportunity is free of charge and requires only your mental awareness to gain priceless treasures. Turn on your mind and notice the opportunities to learn and better yourself as you experience life. This is a principle in and of itself that will greatly enhance your personal development and motivate you in your commitment to excellence in life.

Have you ever gone to a mall or other public setting and people-watched? It's one of my favorite things to do. Just by observing the interactions of others, you can gather so much about communication, social norms, and quality relationships. Right away you'll notice that communication is more effective when people look each other in the eyes when speaking and listening. You may also notice that the dress and appearance of people can influence the impressions of others. Observing others may also give us insight into how a person handles his or her temper. Does body language suggest that someone is in or out of control? Now, these are just a few examples of how much learning we can gain by observing daily life, making connections, and then applying what we learn to our own lives. If we could gain one lesson of knowledge each day and relate that to our lives, how much more effective could we be?

When I was in junior high and high school, I was not a big fan of history. I was bored and didn't find much interest in things like the Boston Tea Party or stories of Davy Crockett. I have since changed my perspective. By learning from history we become aware of both the potential pitfalls and the opportunities of life, thus avoiding unnecessary suffering by reaping the same consequences. This valuable knowledge of events and priceless information can clearly help direct our lives.

Never forget that the world is your classroom and that the knowledge you can gain is limitless. As you come across stories of success from newspaper clippings, books, conversations, etc., create an archive where you can file this valuable information.

I have an archive filing system that has separate folders for each of the five core values faith, relationships, personal development, health, and resources. This way I can categorize the stories I find, making it much easier to locate a newspaper clipping or magazine advertisement in the future. Every piece of information you gather will contribute to your recipe for success, strengthen your core values, and help you overcome potential setbacks.

In recent years the U.S. has faced some financial turmoil. Some say that it is the worst financial crisis we have experienced since the Great Depression. People like my grandmother learned great lessons of self-reliance and sacrifice during the financial hardship of her era. To this day my grandma is careful about turning the lights off, staying out of debt, and planting a vegetable garden. She has not forgotten the pain everyone suffered during that time in history, yet she has wisely applied this knowledge to prepare for the future in case of a similar event. Our ability to glean valuable knowledge from historical events can help minimize and reduce our chances of failure in the future.

After gaining knowledge, you choose to either apply what you've learned or forget about it, pushing it to the back of your brain. This is significant because knowledge in and of itself is of no value unless it is applied. Once knowledge has been applied it becomes wisdom. This is the greatest form of knowledge and has the greatest value and ability to influence our lives. When we live, learn, and apply knowledge, we gain wisdom and life naturally becomes more meaningful and fulfilling.

Success Journal

When you find something that works, write it down. I've made it a habit for more than twenty years to keep what I call a *success journal*. Whenever I learn a principle for success, I write it in this designated journal. Over the years I've recorded thousands of principles I've learned from my own experiences—both successes and failures—and from my observation of others. A success journal should include what you've gained from the experiences of life and how you feel about those experiences. In your success journal you can openly express yourself without reservation, recording your thoughts on how to apply your newfound knowledge to your personal goals and dreams. These principles of success cover many aspects of life, including interpersonal communication, effective time management, proper budgeting of money, attributes of a successful person, natural laws for successful weight loss, etc.

Years ago when I was a financial advisor, I learned some great principles of investing. I would spend countless hours studying stock charts, researching fundamental data, and subscribing to the *Investor's Business Daily* newspaper. My goal was to create a successful system for choosing winning stocks. I learned to look for a long history of earnings success, a pattern or trend the stock had followed over history, and current news of the company. One of the multiple indicators I noted was how much stock the owners and employees owned of the company. I figured that no one knew the company better than the people closest to it. I resolved that if there was a high percentage of ownership within the company of its own stock, these individual buyers were confident in the abilities of their company. This was one of many deciding factors, but it often was a successful indicator of confidence within the company. The best stockbroker is only right 70%–80% of the time, so you try to put the odds in your favor. There is always a degree of uncertainty and risk in the stock market, but identifying successful indicators helps minimize as much risk as possible.

We all can record principles of success in every aspect of life, whether they be principles of investing or principles of effective communication. When we see something that works or is successful, we should write it down. We should also write down when something does not work so that we can be better prepared the next time. As we get into the habit of writing down principles of success in the various aspects of our life, we will be more effective and gain valuable insight.

Success journals offer a vast array of benefits and can be an effective tool in our personal progress and effectiveness. The wisdom and experiences we record will strengthen our resolve to succeed, remind us what is most important in this life, and tell us how we can be most effective. Recording our findings can help us be more effective goal planners, as well as help us crystallize our thoughts and interpret knowledge from life experiences to eventually turn it into wisdom. As we record our feelings, thoughts, and experiences of life in a success journal, we gain valuable information that helps direct our lives.

One such example from my success journal was a personal observation of common characteristics of likeable and successful people. I watched stories of top business executives, saw interviews with professional athletes, and observed people in their natural day-to-day routine. I wanted to see what attributes these seemingly successful people had in common.

After careful observation over an extended period of time, I came to the conclusion that likeable successful people smile a lot, tend to be happy, are upbeat and positive, exude energy, display confidence, are relaxed, rarely complain, can laugh at themselves, look like they are having fun, are teachable, and have an attitude of gratitude.

Another example of something I logged in my success journal was the art of interpersonal communication. I noticed that we can gain effective interpersonal communication from making good eye contact, taking a sincere interest in others (not talking about ourselves), effectively reading others' body language, listening, remembering names, and showing respect for others.

These simple yet effective observations can teach us valuable and effective tools for life. These treasures of daily learning and observance can strengthen our core values and improve our quality of life. As we learn from those who have gone before us and from our own experiences, we are able to avoid some of the same pitfalls and learn what motivates and achieves true success.

Learn the Formulas for Success in Every Component of Life

There is a recipe for success that will unlock our potential in each aspect of life, but we must first decode this formula to tap into its power. My kids often hear me say, "When you obey the law, good things happen. When you don't, bad things happen." I repeat this phrase consistently because I want my kids to realize that when they disobey laws or principles of success, they only hurt themselves. The principles cannot and will not be fooled, but rather they will claim their victim and prize.

Simply put, when it comes to health we know that in order to lose weight, we must burn more calories than we eat. This could be categorized as a law of health or one of our natural laws. We know that this formula works; yet as a country we spend billions of dollars each year trying to shortcut the system with fad diets. These quick-fix solutions may show temporary results, but they come up short of a lasting impact. The formula for success in health is sure—we must pay the price of burning more calories or eating fewer calories to gain the ultimate reward of weight loss. Why do we deviate from what we know will produce a sure result? Because we want the result now without putting in the work. We are trying to reap the harvest without planting the crop, but by law this is impossible. When we fail to pay the price to gain our desired result, we will come up short every time and only rob ourselves of the opportunity to reach our ultimate potential.

So if we know what to do and how to do it, why do we fall into the same traps and pitfalls? Why do we pay others so much money to find a quick fix? Somehow we feel like we can achieve the results and neglect the formula that it is founded upon. Save your money and invest in the principles and formulas that guarantee results. You may feel that it's too painful to pay the price to get what you want, but it will be more painful if your success is short lived because it was founded on false principles. True formulas will bring about sure results as you accompany them with hard work and effort.

The seven formulas I've outlined in this book also apply to the laws of finance. The formula for developing financial independence is not to just make a bunch of money.

We constantly see prolific stars and athletes who get paid an incredible amount of money and yet suffer financially and oftentimes lose it all. How does this happen to someone who makes millions of dollars? The answer is that no matter how much money you make, the formula for financial independence is to spend less than you make. This sounds so simple, but the harsh truth is that we seldom follow this instruction. When we have money, we tend to increase our lifestyle along with it, so we always wonder why we don't have enough and can never get ahead. We try to shortcut the system and put things on credit that we cannot afford, leaving us stressed and in a financial quagmire when the bill comes.

As a financial advisor I worked with many exceptionally talented professionals. I had clients who were brilliant doctors, skilled lawyers, and savvy restaurant owners. I also worked with experienced pilots and some expert mechanical engineers. It surprised me to find that individuals who are so successful career-wise sometimes lack the discipline and wisdom to manage money. Every one of my clients worked very hard at their profession and had applied formulas for success to gain prosperity, but they lacked the same discipline and effort to manage their wealth.

In all the years I worked as a financial advisor, the best advice I could give to others was to not invest more than they could afford to lose and to spend less money than they made. This advice was of far greater value than anything I could have taught them about trading stocks and bonds. These investment vehicles also had their value and importance, and we made and lost money in these efforts, but none of these tools were as effective as my clients' ability to manage their money on a daily basis.

As we apply formulas for success to our relationships with others, we will find positive results just as in the areas of health and finance. Whether we are applying these universal formulas as they pertain to a family member, friend, or stranger, we can connect with others through a proper application of the principle. For example, if you want to build a relationship with your spouse you must forget yourself and serve him or her. While this sounds amazingly simple, we often fail to execute. We can't expect to build a relationship with another individual if all we do is take. It will never work if we try to secure the prize with no effort. You may get what you want in the short-term, but the long-term effects of this misapplication of the formula will take its toll, as evidenced in today's high divorce rate. As we forget ourselves and serve others, we will develop successful, lasting relationships.

Human tendency is to go after our desired result with the least amount of pain as possible. Therefore we fall into the fallacy that we can obtain those results with a quick-fix solution. While we spend great amounts of money and try many other options to obtain the same result without paying the price, the truth is that the formula for success is set, and it cannot be fooled or changed. These principles are timeless and require us to pay a price to gain their reward. The power and results that come from following correct principles are endless, and if we work with them instead of fighting against them, they can help us realize our ultimate dreams and potential.

Successful by Association

Sometimes we sabotage our own success by the way we associate our goals, meaning by the way we erroneously connect success with the negative feelings of pain and suffering. Negative association sets us up for failure and keeps us from even trying to achieve our goals. We must make our ultimate desires clear and associate greater pleasure with the end result than with the pain endured in order to achieve it. Otherwise we link so much pain with accomplishing our goal that we impede ourselves from moving forward in life.

For example, when it comes to health, we all want more energy and to have strong and healthy bodies. When our bodies are young, they can be maintained with less effort and don't feel the wear and tear as much as when we begin to age. This is why we could eat cheeseburgers all the time as teenagers and feel very few side effects. However, as the years go by, these unhealthy habits begin to take their toll and oftentimes manifest themselves in the form of diabetes, cancer, heart disease, and other related sickness and disease. If we knew that the end result could be detrimental and felt the pain ahead of time, I have a feeling we would take better care of ourselves now. There is no doubt we would associate more pain with the sickness and disease than with working out and eating healthy.

Sometimes it can be difficult to see consequences that are so far down the road. However, if we understand formulas for success, we know that all laws result in unpleasant consequences when they are not followed—it's a natural cause and effect. By understanding this principle and pinpointing our ultimate desires, we can link more pleasure with what we really want than the temporary pain with the work it will take to achieve it. The mind is able to produce according to your thoughts.

This same principle applies with material things as well. Take for instance a brand new car. You could run this car ragged and even skip the oil changes and tune-ups, and the car would show very little outward evidence of the neglect. In fact for the first fifty thousand miles, most cars can be maintained with very little consequence, simply needing some tires, adequate oil, and gas in the tank. However, as time goes by, the consequences of not maintaining the car will manifest themselves in various manners. The law cannot be fooled or broken but will in the end exact its debt. The same rule applies in every aspect our lives. Sooner or later the formula will play out, and we will reap its reward or its consequence.

We must train our minds to associate a greater reward with obedience to these natural laws than to the pain endured from their neglect. The way we can achieve this is by focusing on our goals and following the formula for success with a knowledge that the end result will be far greater than the sure consequence that would follow otherwise. Looking at the end goal can give us greater clarity on what we really want to achieve. By reshaping our thoughts to associate pleasure and reward with our desired result, we can overcome anything in our path that would prevent us from achieving our goal. Remember your ultimate pleasure is living your dreams, so choose to associate your way to success.

When I was young, I looked at certain rules or laws as restrictive and confining. Whether it was a curfew or a dress codes, some rules seemed like their only purpose was to limit what I could do. I learned from my own failures that laws are not there to restrict us but to actually keep us free. The rule of a curfew is a great way to reduce the amount of trouble a teenager can get into. The way we dress, I learned, really does send a message to others, either good or bad. When we eat healthy, we have a greater chance of being free of sickness, but when we consume harmful things, our options are reduced and our chances for negative consequences increase. Rules actually keep us from suffering negative consequences that might have come from breaking the law. It is when we don't live the law or the rule that our options are limited and our freedom is reduced.

Once I realized how laws set us free rather than restrict us, I decided to tap into that power rather than kick against it. There is no shortcut or way around success. When we become aware that it's through obedience to natural laws of success that we are set free, we will discover a power that will allow us to accomplish anything we desire. This power may not come instantaneously, but with patience we will get the lasting result of our hard work.

Patience Brings the Greater Reward

In this day and age it's rare to find anyone who enjoys being patient. We get frustrated when our high speed Internet won't connect fast enough to give us a restaurant address or background on an unknown term. Remember when we had to use a phonebook or an encyclopedia to get this information? Our technologically deprived way of life even fifteen years ago would drive some people crazy today. How quickly we adjust to the fast pace and forget how it feels to wait. But as crazy as it may sound, there can be pleasure in patience.

Many of us get impatient and look so far down the road that we fail to recognize our incremental achievements. I once worked with a young man who was struggling with life and felt overwhelmed by its challenges. We looked at his circumstances and talked about a plan of action. He wondered why he was so unhappy and couldn't break the shackles he felt weighing him down. I asked about his schedule and about what he accomplished in a day. He wasn't going to school, wasn't working, and didn't have any goals in his future. We discussed the consequences associated with having no plan and the hopelessness that would follow anyone who had no goals. We talked about his options, noting the outcome of the different paths he could choose from.

I told him, "You could lie around the house, curl up in a ball, and give up on life, which will give you no ultimate pleasure whatsoever. You would become lazy, out of shape, and slow to reach any potential educational or financial goals that would benefit you. Or you could get a job, go to school, and go after some forgotten dreams. Either way, life is going to move forward with or without you, so get on the train or you'll miss your next stop."

This young man was so overcome by his challenges that he didn't realize he had a choice in the matter. For so long he'd felt crippled by a fear of failure: he feared that if he went to school he would get bad grades; if he asked out a girl she would turn him down; or if he got a job he would get fired. He wanted to be successful but was afraid to fail. We discussed the fact that success is not the absence of failure but rather the ability to get up time and time again until you succeed. You never fail unless you fail to get up. All successful people I know have failed and failed more than once.

This young man began to see that his choices were the result of his emotional condition and soon realized that he was not just a robotic tin man destined for misery. He went back to school, starting dating again, and received a lucrative job opportunity. He began to take charge of his life, applying

Common Denominators for Success

the Seven Formulas for Success to strengthen his resolve and allow him to dream again and accomplish his goals. If we will learn to be patient and realize that success hardly ever happens instantly, we will witness the universal laws at work in our behalf. Success usually happens as we patiently and persistently get up again and again after being knocked down, until we claim the prize.

Sometimes we are too hard on ourselves, thinking we're pathetic for not yet having reached our goal when we barely got the new habit rolling. We don't give ourselves the credit we deserve—remember, the pyramids of Egypt weren't built in a night. With persistent obedience to the laws of success, we can obtain those dreams we desire. Take one step at a time, keeping your eye on the mark, and you will arrive at your destination. Don't focus on how long it takes, just trust that you'll eventually get there. Baby steps lead to big steps, and big steps lead to big dreams.

Recap: Results Stem from Natural Laws

Natural laws govern our universe and enable us to enjoy consistency in choices and consequences, learn from the world around us, and apply what we learn to better our lives and the lives of those around us. The more we learn, the better we can understand that results stem from natural laws adhered to or broken, and the more frequently we'll notice laws in action all around us.

Formulas such as laws of finance, laws of health, and laws of relationships govern our choices. We can't override the system or bribe the guard; we must work and focus and be patient in our efforts. And then if we are persistent, we will get what we want out of life. Natural laws are fixed and will never cheat us. If we channel our thoughts, words, and actions so that they focus on our limitless potential, choose to succeed, and then take action, we will see positive changes in our lives and achieve our greatest dreams. We were not meant to just survive but rather to thrive and reach our highest potential.

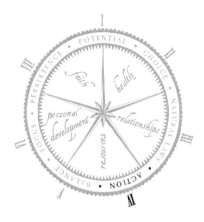

Formula 4:

Action = Results

Wisdom is knowledge applied.

Converting Knowledge into Action

As we start to see that all things are founded on laws and that lasting success comes only through our obedience to those natural laws, it will be instinctive for us to apply this knowledge to our lives to see if it really works. When we put our knowledge to use, it then becomes wisdom and has a useful purpose to help generate results. The knowledge I'm talking about isn't just secular knowledge; I'm referring to any knowledge we gain that can be applied toward good. I say "toward good" because I don't consider knowledge applied for a bad use to be wisdom, as that would thwart the very meaning of its intended function.

When you really think about it, knowledge does nothing for us if we don't apply what we learn. For instance, where is the benefit in a carpenter learning his trade if he never actually creates anything out of wood? How about the engineer who goes to school and learns about the laws that govern the construction of a building, but then she never puts that education to use? How effective would this engineer be if she had no hands-on building experience but wanted to teach others how to build? Could she really be an effective engineering instructor without having ever implemented those principles herself? Knowledge serves no purpose if we don't take action and apply what we learn.

Students for Life

Learning is the portal through which we gain a clear vision of who we are and what we can become. A formal education serves as a useful building block of knowledge to teach us how to learn and motivate us to keep learning. What we learn in a formal classroom should be just the beginning of our pursuit for wisdom. After I graduated from college, I had a better perspective on life and a more complete idea of who I was, realizing I was just beginning my life's education. As I continued into careers and experienced life, gathering more knowledge and wisdom along the way, I could confidently state that the learning I had done outside the formal classroom had taught me so much more than I could've ever imagined. Never stop learning.

I've seen many people in life who hide behind the veil of their education and, by so doing, curtail their ability to continue learning. Once they have their credential of authority, they stop the very process that motivated their purpose. I've discovered that education and learning are a lifelong quest, so look to those who use their education as a springboard to continue learning—those are the stalwarts in the pursuit of success. Learning is a continuous and wonderful process that stimulates progress and development in every aspect of our lives. Use your five core values as guides to keep focused on the most important aspects of life to increase your faith, improve your relationships, strengthen your personal worth, better your health, and develop your resource management skills. The moment we think we've learned it all is the moment we stop progressing.

The act of applying knowledge and gaining wisdom is what perpetuates our success and drives us forward in the pursuit of excellence. The exciting news is that there is an endless supply of wisdom to be gained in this life and that the acquisition of this wisdom can and should be an exhilarating and lifelong adventure. We can uncover treasures of wisdom every day if we recognize the correct principles and universal laws all around us, and apply this knowledge to our daily lives.

At age twenty-two, I took a sales position to pay my way through college. This job taught me effective communication skills, and I instantly became fascinated with the effect that successful interpersonal communication skills could have on building relationships. Having an interest in personal development to begin with, this field sparked my interest, and I became an avid student in the art of communication. I learned that the way we communicate influences everything we do in this life. Effective communication influences our family life, careers, health, faith, hobbies, interests, and pretty much everything we do. Because communication is so vital to success, I wanted to master this art. I learned that interpersonal communication was comprised of the following components:

eye contact, facial expressions, voice, body language, and attitude. Most of the messages we send to others have less to do with our actual words and more to do with the way we communicate those words.

After starting the sales job, I decided to read a book by world-famous communication consultant Roger Ailes. His book *You Are the Message* validates the components of interpersonal communication listed above and breaks down the secrets of the master communicators. That summer I applied what I learned about communication to the sale of my product. I knew that I could sell only something that I believed in. I let this confidence and attitude reflect in making good eye contact with others, letting the enthusiasm show in my face and in my voice, and using hand gestures to make my points. It worked! That summer I ended up setting a company record in sales and, by so doing, put myself through college. I even had leftover money for some dates. I learned a valuable lesson in communication that summer, and this wisdom has been an interest and a value to me since.

Successful people all through the ages have sought to apply wisdom and correct principles in their lives. Confucius, an influential Eastern philosopher who was responsible for much of the foundation for Asian culture, devoted his life to learning. He was one who applied correct principles and pursued natural laws, which contributed to his ethical behavior and moral character. This quest has made him one of the most influential philosophers of our day. He was a true lifelong scholar who discovered countless treasures of wisdom and spent his life in study and purposeful application. The world was his classroom.

WBDA Principle

As students for life, we will begin to recognize laws at work all around us. One such law I've discovered that relates to every aspect of life is what I call the *WBDA Principle*. This stands for: "Want it. Believe it. Do it. Achieve it." Now, these four steps may sound easy, but this formula actually takes unbelievable discipline to master. The WBDA Principle is the key to following through on all your goals, so engrain this acronym in your mind to help you remember the four key elements to success.

Want It

The "W" in WBDA stands for *want*, referring to the things that you want most in life—your priorities, your five core values. So *do* you know what you really want out of life? I pose this question because sometimes we mask our true desires behind superficial answers to help alleviate the pain of not achieving our real dreams. Oftentimes we settle or become complacent in what we want because we lose hope, thinking that what we really want is not within our grasp or that it would be too painful to obtain. Quit selling yourself short and start living again.

Have you ever peeled back an onion and noticed how many layers it has? We're just like that onion. Sometimes we must peel back layer after layer in our own lives to get to the core of what we really want. The layers on the outside are composed of self-doubt, fear, procrastination, and many other roadblocks to success. But the point is that we are like onions with many layers of obstacles that prevent us from identifying what it is that we really want.

What are the layers that stop you from reaching your dreams? Do you feel like too much of your life has gone by and now it's too late to change? Do you feel like you don't have the time or energy to accomplish your desires? Do you feel like you've already tried and your attempts were unsuccessful? Put the past in perspective and learn from it; visualize the future ahead and prepare for it; and focus on the present and live it! There's much hope in knowing that it's not where we've been that matters but rather where we are today. It's never too late to make a change.

Let me also say that peeling back the onion requires some deep self-introspection. When we start to peel back the layers, we begin to see our wants and desires from a new perspective that we may not have originally seen. For example, some people feel like money will solve all their problems, and then when they gain that prosperity, they wonder why they aren't happy. Peeling back the layers of life means getting to the very core of what we want and not just the superficial exterior. When we say we want financial resources, what is it that we really want? Do we want the material aspects of perceived joy or do we want something more? I am not suggesting that a goal of a material nature is bad, but rather the reason we desire financial prosperity may wear many masks. For me, the value of financial prosperity is the time that it can afford me to pursue my real wants and passions. I believe that time is the real value of money. So when I say peel back the onion, I mean get down to the very reason why you desire something.

To peel back your layers, clear your mind of all the confusion and busyness of life for a moment. What is it that you really want out of life? What are your goals? These are your innermost dreams, so let your imagination run wild for a moment and take away all barriers. Get down to the very heart of your goals and freely write down and contemplate your ultimate dreams.

Oftentimes I go into the mountains for this process so that I can be free from cell phones, people, and other distractions. I close my eyes and listen to the peaceful sounds of nature that surround me, and for just a moment I feel like I have a refuge where my spirit can be free and where I can get clear on what I really want out of life. It's important to contemplate in a place and time when you are free from distractions and time constraints. You need this time to let your creativity flow and your spirit soar.

After I've had some time to contemplate the dreams and aspirations in my mind, I write these feelings and goals in a journal or planner—what will eventually be my *blueprint for success*, which we'll talk about in chapter 8. I think of the five core values—faith, relationships, personal development, health, and resources—and decide what I want from each one. We will talk more about balance in the next chapter, but I'll note that these core values touch on all aspects of life that bring us balance and influence our minds, bodies, and spirits. It is important to identify what you want in life in each area in order to incorporate a balance that will fulfill your life and allow you to reach your potential as a well-rounded individual.

I remember when I was in college I had a roommate who was getting ready to propose to his girlfriend. I asked him, "Is this the girl of your dreams?" He replied that no, she wasn't but that he figured she was the best he could get. I felt pained at his response and his willingness to give up on finding the woman best for him. How often do we cut ourselves short of what we really want because we don't think we deserve better? For one of the most important decisions in his life, this roommate was prepared to settle for a woman he felt would take him. How unfair was this to both him and his girlfriend? He deserved to be with the person of his dreams, someone he truly loved and someone who made him feel like he was the luckiest man alive.

My roommate and I ended up having a lengthy discussion about this topic. He asked me what I was looking for in a companion, so I pulled out a list of the main qualities I wanted in my future companion—at the time I was still in pursuit of my wife. He said, "Do you think it's realistic that you'll actually end up with the person you think is best for you?" I said, "Absolutely, and I am not going to settle for anything less." Now, I never said that the person I was looking for had to be perfect, but I did say she had to be perfect for me. To hope to qualify for this type of companion, I knew I too had to be living up to the same standards I desired in a wife. I knew that I had plenty of imperfections myself, but I had to feel like, if given a choice, the person I would end up with was *the* choice of my heart.

Sometimes we fail to identify what we really want because we lack the clarity to know who we really are and what we are capable of. We see only our own faults and lose perspective of what our real potential is. We settle for mediocre goals because our perspective is foggy and limited, so we lose hope. This is exactly what my roommate experienced, and if this sounds familiar to you too, wake up and see life through the lens that anything is possible. My roommate eventually did just this and ended up with a wonderful woman who reflected those qualities he really wanted in a partner. We are limited only by our own narrow beliefs of ourselves, so identify those goals in life that you really want—those goals that could be yours in your greatest dreams—and then pursue them with vigor and never give up on them.

Believe It

Now, a desire is just the beginning of the formula. After we have the want in mind, we must *believe* that we can actually attain it. Often we sabotage ourselves, thinking that we aren't good enough to have something we want, or convince ourselves that it would require too much work and effort. Whatever your Kryptonite, don't let it get to you! Believing means taking ownership of your choices, which indirectly means taking ownership of your thoughts, words, and actions. Believing means being able to visualize yourself realizing your dreams and accomplishing your greatest desires by taking action to achieve them. When we believe that we can have whatever we want as long as it is based on correct principles, we gain confidence in our ability to make our dreams a reality.

Believing is critical in achieving our goals and being successful. How do we increase our ability to believe we can achieve our goals and dreams? One way to increase your belief in yourself is by applying the As If Principle, which we discussed in chapter 1. It's the idea of writing down those things we want to accomplish as if we've already done them, thus putting our mind in a state of success and action. We've also talked about the power of visualization and how our ability to visualize our success can enhance our effectiveness. And we've also emphasized the importance of our thoughts and how those thoughts influence our results. By surrounding ourselves with positive influences, we can change our way of thinking to eliminate negativity and start to believe we can accomplish anything we set our minds to.

Mastering our thoughts is similar to strengthening our physical bodies. If we don't exercise, our muscles deteriorate and wither. Years ago I severed my patella tendon while playing basketball. Within weeks after surgery, being unable to exercise the muscles in that leg, I began to notice considerable atrophy. It literally left my injured leg half the size of the healthy one. When we don't exercise our mental muscles, we lose strength and ability to properly use thought mastery. As we exercise these mental muscles by taking responsibility for our thoughts, we gain greater capacity for powerful results. Just as I regained the size and strength in my injured leg, we also can regain the power and use of our minds through proper exercise of our thoughts.

By taking charge of our thoughts, we are making a significant step toward gaining positive results in every aspect of life. We will become what we choose to think about, so if you want to be successful, think success. Like a magnet, we draw to us what we choose to think about. The ability to succeed is in the eye of the believer—you will accomplish what you think you can. What you believe becomes your reality, and your reality becomes your life. Therefore if you understand that you can make of your life whatever you choose, then choose to believe in your dreams.

Part of believing you can do something is clearly understanding why you want this goal. Why is it so important for you to achieve *this*, of all things? We've already talked about identifying your ultimate wants and believing that you can achieve them; now we're ready to take action to gain the reward. The *why* behind what you do from here on out will make all the difference.

It's often valuable to think of the consequences of not achieving your goal, because then you quickly see that you'd be crazy to not make it happen. You realize that the ultimate pleasure in accomplishing your goal would be greater than the pain. For instance, if you want to strengthen your relationship with your kids, what would be the consequence of failing to do so? Not being close to your children; feeling a deep void in your life from not prioritizing your children into your life; feeling lonely and unfulfilled in your later years; or your kids feeling like you never took time for them. These potential consequences are unquestionably more painful than dedicating time now to getting to know your children on a regular basis.

I think we often justify our actions to minimize our responsibility and thus alleviate our guilt about being unsuccessful. We say, for example, that we are working hard for our family. While this is often true, I know from experience how easy it is to use work and other diversions as excuses to justify what we are not doing. I've been guilty myself of justifying my work by saying, "The reason I work so hard is for the family," as if to excuse myself for not spending more time with them. Somehow it made me feel better about myself and allowed me to rationalize neglecting something that was a greater priority. If we want to put our kids first, or anyone or anything for that matter, and develop a close bond, our *why* must reflect that reasoning. Our *why* must be greater than our excuses for not accomplishing our goal.

The *why* for which we do something must be so strong that we're willing to sacrifice whatever it takes to realize this goal, even if it requires the sacrifice of our own pride at times. We must be honest with ourselves and not hide behind excuses or blame our circumstances on external factors, but rather put those things that matter most first in our lives.

This same principle works for staying healthy. My wife and I work out together every morning for one hour. There are days when we're both tired, and it sounds good to sleep in, especially in the winter when it's snowing; however, we realize that if we sleep in and don't exercise we will want to do that the next day. We also know that if we sleep in, we will have a greater tendency to not eat as well, since it's just one day, right? And we know that if we get in the habit of not exercising and eating poorly, our health will suffer. These days heart disease and diabetes are so prevalent, even among children, and the consequences for neglecting our health are too painful to ignore. When we look at the big picture we realize that, although getting up early can be tough, ultimately we know that the benefits of staying in good shape far outweigh the alternative. The *why* for which we sacrifice some extra sleep is of far greater importance in the long run than if we didn't work out.

If things came easily and were free, there would be no need to believe. Reaching your ultimate wants in life requires you to sacrifice and pay a price, but I promise that if you establish a significant *why*, your ability to believe in yourself will be magnified and solidified. Keep your eye on the big picture of your desired goal, and you will find the willpower and faith to fight through the pain to victory. This victory and the pleasure you gain will be worth the price you pay, so when you first believe you can do something, make your *why* huge.

Do It

This brings us to the "D" in the WBDA Principle, which stands for *do*. Once we've identified our goals and believe that they can be ours, we now have the energy, courage, and motivation to take action. By taking action and doing those things that will help us achieve our dreams, we put into motion the very essential ingredient that produces the result. Most of us know that this formula works, that deliberate action founded on true desires and unwavering faith has to result in success, but are we willing to make these choices and pay the price to obtain the ultimate reward?

Thinking and believing you are financially stable will not make money instantly appear in your wallet, but it will motivate you to do something to make it a reality. Belief without action equals failure; belief with action equals results. Success requires not just hard work, but hard work with a plan. Let's say you identify your want as, "Lose weight to better my health and increase my stamina." You honestly believe you can be healthier, but then when it comes time to perform, you collapse on the couch every day after work, flip on the television, and open the freezer to enjoy some microwaveable goodness (i.e., lard). If this is your daily routine, you will never attain your goal; however, if you do something by creating a plan of attack and then following through with your plan, you will lose weight and accomplish your desire to be healthier.

So in order for the WBDA Principle to work, the *do* part requires a plan: how will you get what you want? So, for example, if you want to be a successful real estate agent, you must put specific tasks in place to merit this prize. You'll need to make so many calls per day, access so many referrals, do so many visits with "for sale by owners," talk to new builders about new home construction, or research raw land prices in the area. You must set up a plan that you can execute, asking yourself, "What is required to meet your long-term goal of being the top agent? Where do you want to be in a year, and what do you need to do today that will help accomplish the goals of tomorrow?" You must put much thought and questioning and planning into the *do* part of the WBDA Principle for it to lead to lasting success.

As you plan how to accomplish a goal, think of efficiency and not just busyness. A person can stay busy doing almost anything, but to be effective he or she must work hard and smart. If you are focused and effective in how you accomplish your tasks, you will accomplish more in two hours than most do in a whole day. A person who goes to the office and spends his or her day checking e-mails, having social lunches, and playing golf is not effective. There is a time and place for all things, but if you hope to reach your financial goals as they pertain to a career, you must work hard and smart. You can measure effectiveness in one way—results.

In order to obtain results, you must have a plan for success and then follow through. By establishing a blueprint for success, you will have a road map to keep you on course and move you one step closer to your goals. First of all, any plan of action must include to-do lists, day-to-day goals, and long-term goals. By breaking your goal into increments, you will be able to note your progress and keep your eye on the ultimate prize. As you come up with bite-size goals, you will also help eliminate the tendency to feel overwhelmed from attempting to consume the whole pie at one time. Take it piece by piece, and eventually you will devour your goal and be victorious.

A second key to creating an effective plan of attack is personalizing it so that the goals are attainable. Start simple if you need to, but start somewhere. Think about your strengths and weaknesses. Do some brainstorming. Think about what you are most willing to give up, what you're sure will work, and how quickly you want to see results. Base your plan of attack on a few short-term and long-term goals that will lead you to your dream, try out your plan, and if something isn't working, make improvements. If your plan is working and you're no longer being challenged as much, take it up a notch and push yourself a little more.

So, for example, if you feel like your goals under your core value of health need improvement, you could change your day-to-day diet plan to allow one serving of sweets a week instead of one serving of sweets a day. The most important thing about creating a plan is that you make it realistic so that it helps you move toward your goal. When it comes to diet, my food plan is to eat really healthy Monday through Friday and then take the weekend off to give myself a break and allow myself some liberties. I find that by doing this, I am reenergized when Monday rolls around, and it gives me a reward to look forward to on the weekends. Without a plan I guarantee that you will fall back into your old ways regardless of how much you want to and believe you can change.

A third vital part of creating a plan of attack is holding yourself accountable. My short- and long-term goals have action items, or numerical goals, attached to them. For example, my short-term goal may be to exercise daily, but my long-term goal may be to weigh 180 pounds. I keep these goals in my planner, but the more reminders you have, the better. Putting them on a mirror or in plain sight around your house or office would be helpful. Also, sharing these goals with a close friend or loved one breeds a sense of accountability. As we openly verbalize our goals to others, our refined focus will enable us to achieve the end result.

Committing to a plan is not always easy, but every worthwhile goal requires sacrifice. Surely we can't expect to gain the best results in life with little to no effort. You will need to remind yourself of this fact when you're getting up at 5 a.m. to work out, or when you're pulling sixty-hour-work weeks to climb the corporate ladder, or when you're scrupulously saving every penny so that you can pay for college. Whatever goal you desire will demand that you pay a price, but the prize will be worth the fight. So keep in mind that if the components *want* and *believe* are separated from *do*, the *achieve* will never happen.

Achieve It

The derivative of the WBDA Principle is the "A," which represents *achieve*—the ultimate reward of wanting, believing, and doing. Achieving a dream requires detailed planning to determine when during each day, week, or month you will dedicate time to accomplishing these plans. Decide your schedule in advance so that you dedicate time to accomplishing your goals. Make sure that your how-to list is filled with practical items that you can schedule and fit into your day. Executing these items will require conscious time management and organization. Stay focused and on task, and you will succeed.

A plan is useless without time management and will never lead to achievement. Unless you dedicate the time necessary to meet both your short- and long-term goals, you'll be detoured by the many distractions of life. The mistake we most often make when setting goals is not having a plan. We may say we want to do something, but we never solidify that desire by listing what is required of our time and energy on a day-to-day basis. Maybe you can hear yourself telling a friend, "I'm going to get on a budget. Yeah, I really need to stop spending so much." Then when your friend asks you when you're going to create your budget, you say something like, "I don't know. It's just something I really know I should do." This is a frivolous goal. Unless you actually plug that desire into the seven formulas laid out in this book, you will never change your spending habits or else you'll try to be frugal for a couple shopping trips before giving up. If you really want to get on a budget, make your *why* huge. Map out a hardcopy plan. Be consistent. Be specific. Make room for your to-dos and make your dream a reality.

When you execute your goals and do what you promised yourself you would do, you gain greater confidence in your ability to succeed. Your self-esteem and self-respect increase, and your integrity is strengthened. You come to know that when you say you're going to do something, you know it will get done. This quality is most valued because you will become someone who can be counted on, and others will respect you for that. You will know that a planned goal is a goal that will be met. Effective people execute and take action.

I try to instill this quality in my children when I make them promises. They know that when dad says he's going to do something, he'll follow through. I've gone to extreme measures to ensure that my kids know they can count on me. One day I promised my kids that I would get them a treat at the store for cleaning their rooms. As I was telling them bedtime stories late that night, my kids reminded me of the promise I had made. We had gotten busy and by the time they reminded me, it was really late. My kids said, "Daddy, you always keep your promises and do what you say you'll do." So I said, "Get your shoes on; we're going to the store for treats." As we went downstairs, my wife looked confused and asked what we were doing. I said, "A promise is a promise."

There will be times when something comes up that wasn't scheduled in your planner, and your time and attention will be needed elsewhere. For example, you may be heading out the door to the gym for your scheduled workout, and a friend calls you with news that she just lost her father. You value your friend and recognize the need to comfort and support her in this time of crisis. Be prepared to be flexible and prioritize your goals so that you always put the things that matter most first.

Positive results of our actions stem from successfully applying knowledge and adhering to natural laws. In this case the natural law is the WBDA Principle: Want it. Believe it. Do it. Achieve it. Universal principles have existed for people from all periods of time just as they exist for us today—you can take any accomplishment in this world and trace it back to this formula. Now, some people may gain momentary results by taking a shortcut or opting for a quick fix, but we gain lasting results only through proper application of this natural law.

Before the 1950s, everyone thought that running a four-minute mile was humanly impossible, but athlete Roger Bannister *wanted* to break that record, *believed* he could do it, set a course of *action*, and *achieved* it. Bannister didn't see a limiting barrier but rather saw only what was possible, and in 1954 ran a 3:59 minute mile to shock the world. Bannister was the first person to break the record, but many other people quickly did the same once they knew it was possible. The record today is 3:26—thirty-four seconds less than what was once thought to be impossible.

Another example of someone who applied the WBDA Principle was a man by the name of Walt Disney. Born in 1901, Disney was determined to perfect the art of animation despite the financial setbacks of the Great Depression. When most people were crippled in fear during the worst economic time in American history, Disney was pioneering the animation world. Disney identified what he wanted, and despite his poor financial circumstances, he believed in his dream of bringing families together through animation and entertainment. Disney produced more than one hundred films, created the legendary animated characters of Mickey Mouse and Donald Duck, and was responsible for the world-renowned theme park Disneyland.

Disney dreamed big and knew what he wanted. He believed he could attain his dream despite the obstacles before him. He had a plan of attack, and he executed that plan until those dreams became a reality, clearly implementing the principle of WBDA. He touched the lives of millions with his vision and determination. This rags-to-riches story shows the resilience of the human spirit and that dreams really can come true.

Whether you want to break a four-minute mile, attain financial independence, or strengthen your marriage, the WBDA Principle works and will help you achieve your dreams. Look to successful people all around you and identify the natural laws they followed to achieve their dreams. When we expand our vision to what is possible and properly apply natural laws, such as the WBDA Principle, we can achieve what once seemed impossible.

Redefining Your Goals

Over time your values and priorities may change to some degree. There is no harm in evaluating your progress and redefining your goals; in fact, this shows great wisdom. As we develop and progress, we will change. Sometimes that change reshapes our blueprint for success, and sometimes it helps us find a better and more effective way to go after our goals. Our values may also change in order of importance. This is okay, and you should embrace these positive changes and allow them to shape your life for the good.

As a young man I was completely focused on sports. I played basketball, baseball, track, and almost any other sport that existed. I would play these sports from the moment I was done with school until I went to bed. I learned fantastic principles of life through sports and gained an incredibly close bond with my father, as he was fully involved with my participation in athletics. As I've grown older, I still love sports as both a spectator and participant, but with a young family of four children, I now find greater value in my time spent with my kids than playing sports. Each stage of our lives summons different needs, so be flexible as new priorities enter your life and require more of your time. I still spend time staying in shape, but I keep my priorities in a more balanced perspective and now use my time to incorporate the family I didn't have twenty years ago.

As we go through life, it's naturally part of the process to redefine our goals and reevaluate our priorities. We should be spending time every week reviewing where we are and where we want to be. This planning process will help us to be more effective people and to live a more balanced and healthy life.

Recap: Action Begets Results

We gain wisdom in life as we act upon our knowledge. Learning is the kindling and action is the match, and together they produce the fire of change and results in our lives. Taking action is what gives knowledge its usefulness and power. As we apply this principle of converting knowledge into action, we can and will achieve results in every aspect of our lives.

We can practice applying our knowledge by implementing the WBDA Principle—"Want it. Believe it. Do it. Achieve it."—which guides us step-by-step toward success. We must first identify what we really want in life so that we have direction. Next we have to believe that our desire is attainable and make our *why* bigger than any amount of pain or sacrifice. If our *why* isn't big enough, there is nothing to fuel our action. Then we must put a plan of action in place to guide our daily choices and short- and long-term goals. And finally we must execute the plan by strategically planning when we can work toward achieving our dream. Wisdom requires us to identify what we really want, believe that we can achieve that goal, create a plan of action that will merit that reward, and execute the plan.

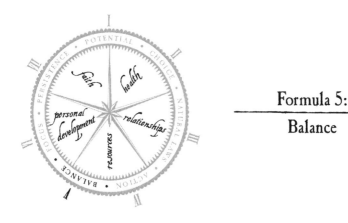

Formula 5:
Balance

Real success is the consistent application of correct principles in every aspect of life.

Diversify Your Life

Too many times we devote all our energies to one aspect of life at the cost of other valuable priorities. Just as we would never put all our money into only one stock for an investment, we too must diversify our lives so as to maintain a healthy and successful balance to life. If we are out of synch and are neglecting one aspect of life, it can have a destructive domino effect that spreads to all other areas, keeping us from reaching our full potential.

When I was working as a stockbroker and advising people on how to invest their money, I recognized that while it is beneficial to instruct people how to best invest their money, it was more important that they know how to diversify their *life* portfolio rather than their *financial* portfolio. I realized that our ability to diversify our lives and prioritize those values of utmost importance is the most valuable investment we could ever make. The greatest stock pick of all time pales in comparison to what we can do with a winning life portfolio. Although financial success can certainly enhance life experiences and provide meaningful opportunities, there is so much more. Financial success is only one component, and if the other vital areas of life are not in synch, then this financial attainment will mean nothing.

Real success is consistent application of correct principles in every aspect of life. Diversifying our lives, or in other words having a balanced life, is critical to our health, success, and overall well-being. Trying to fit all we need to do in a day is challenging and leaves us saying, "I wish there were more hours in a day!" The truth is that even if we had more hours, many of us would spend the extra time doing the same tasks that we do now. Being able to balance our lives is reflected in our time-management skills. We can and should maintain this balance if we are to live a full life and achieve the greatest success.

The concept of diversifying our lives focuses on prioritizing our time among the five core values of life:

1. Faith
2. Relationships
3. Personal Development
4. Health
5. Resources (Time and Money)

When diversifying our lives, I find it helps to categorize the five values into two groups. Faith, relationships, and personal development are the first three values, which I call *critical values.* These values reflect our need to belong and progress in this life, and they define who we are and how we interact with others. They establish our road map of integrity and social interaction. The other two needs I call *maintenance values.* These two values, health and resources (time and money), allow us to enjoy a greater quality of life and afford us the time to spend fulfilling our three critical values. Again, all of us share these universal values, and they are essential for maximizing our quality of life and allowing us the freedom to pursue our dreams.

We must diversify our lives to keep all five of these core values in harmony or the results can be catastrophic. In this chapter, I will explain the importance of diversifying our lives to maintain this balance and the benefits that come when we do. I will also discuss the consequences and effects that accompany an unbalanced life. Finding balance to life is at the core of reaching our potential, living out our dreams, and ultimately being successful.

Value 1: Faith

Faith is composed of beliefs, knowledge, and attitude. No matter what religious affiliation you claim or don't claim, we all share the value of faith. Each of us has faith, whether you realize it or not, and when we exercise that faith, we extend our belief in something that we cannot see. This faith may be in the results of morning exercise, for example. You may not initially see the weight loss or feel the added energy, but you work out because you have the faith that if you do, you will eventually see a difference. Our lives operate every day on our faith. The very fact that you go to sleep at night and expect to see the sun the next day is faith in its simplest form.

Our faith starts with a belief. A simple belief then gives us a desire to experiment upon its usefulness, which is the infancy stage of this belief. In fact let's first talk about the faith of a child. Small children believe that their parents will feed and dress them. They experiment upon the usefulness of this method by crying until their needs are fulfilled. When they see the experiment is successful, they start becoming somewhat savvy to its usefulness, illustrating how we all learn from infancy how to apply our faith in different situations.

As we grow we gain more knowledge, and we experience the pleasures and pains in the application of our faith. I remember touching the bottom of an iron when I was six years old. That brief but memorable experience caused me immense pain. I learned quickly that touching a hot iron brought bad results, and I never did it again. As we get older we have greater choices to make and more opportunities to apply our faith through experimentation. When we see fruitful results we are strengthened by that success, which acts as a positive reinforcement. We are then more likely to want the same positive results in the future.

When we apply our faith it eventually becomes wisdom; the very nature of the word "apply" insinuates taking action. We may not even realize that we're applying our faith, but if we take a moment to analyze our lives as a whole and our actions in a given day, I suspect that we would see an abundance of faith. Faith is the first value we will discuss in regard to diversifying our lives because faith is the foundation to everything we do in life. If we are to be successful, we must have faith that as we successfully apply these principles we will get our desired results.

Faith unlocks the results behind the door of life, but we must turn the knob. We can't see the benefits hidden behind the door until after we've applied our faith by taking action on our beliefs. When we act upon our beliefs we trigger that formula for success that unveils the potential found within each one of us. Whether it is going to work every day or spending time with our spouse or learning a new skill, we are applying faith that by accomplishing these tasks, we will be financially stable or have a happier marriage or experience a greater sense of self. When you go to work you have the faith that if you do your job, you will get paid, since we generally don't receive our wages until we have put forth the effort. This value of faith holds true in every sense—we cannot expect to receive the reward without paying the price.

The universal principle of faith directly applies to the core value of health, for example. We gain the results of weight loss by first putting our faith in the knowledge that lasting results come only through adhering to natural laws, which means paying the price of working out and eating right. Sometimes we may try to take a shortcut by doing fad diets in an attempt to get the immediate reward, but without the proper application of correct principles, we will never attain lasting success.

I have a friend who was experimenting with a quick-fix diet program. He said, "It's great! I eat all the bacon, cheese, and meat that I want, and I don't even need to work out." He lost a lot of weight in four weeks and looked slim. He thought he had found a magic formula that defied the system of success and didn't require a price to be paid. However, the side effects caught up with him, and he suffered a heart attack some time later. This was a sad situation, and it's not to say that the same thing will necessarily happen to you, but it demonstrates that we cannot shortcut correct principles. Proper application of correct principles brings successful results, and the neglect, shortcut, or failure to observe these principles brings adverse consequences. Some of these effects show up years down the road, but make no mistake about it, the principle will deliver its prize or prisoner.

Our faith in correct principles is the key to successful results in relationships as well. Statistical data show that failed relationships are at an all-time high. In recent years we've failed to apply correct principles to our faith in relationships. We often shortcut these principles when we hope for a strong bond of marriage or other healthy relationships but are not willing to pay the price of letting go of pride or giving up selfishness. This inability to properly associate with others leads to numerous problems and great unhappiness.

The world is seeing firsthand the ill effects of improper application of correct principles as they pertain to financial matters. In the United States, 2008 was the beginning of economic turmoil because we had over extended ourselves as a country and had looked to shortcut the principle of accumulating wealth. These consequences have manifest themselves in the improperly inflated values of homes and land without justification. We have loaned more money than a property is worth and have extended loans beyond people's ability to pay such debt. Some experienced wealth overnight, and some lost it just as quickly. We have improperly applied principles of success and relied on quick-fix solutions, and are now facing the harsh realities of poor financial decisions.

Many of us are victims of these consequences without merit, yet we see the overall detriment of our mismanagement as a whole.

Faith is the foundation of real success because we must have the hope and patience that if we apply correct principles in the right way, the reward will follow. And it will! Applying this faith is not always easy; in fact, it can test us to the very core. However, the results will prove themselves in the end and will be worth the price of admission. We all have our own unique set of challenges. Whether these challenges involve a failed marriage, the desire to accumulate wealth, or a goal to lose weight, the value of faith is at the very heart of hope of something more. Faith lifts us and allows us to see beyond ourselves and strive for something better. Faith gives us the motivation to change, take action, take charge, and live our dreams.

We strengthen our faith as we apply its power. When we add action to our hope and gain results, our faith and confidence grow. We can strengthen that faith in every aspect of life whether it is in spiritual matters that connect us with God or a higher power, our relationships with others, personal pursuit of dreams, our health, or our management of time and money. Faith plays a key role in each of these components and priorities of life. We can increase our faith by experimenting upon its application and discovering the rewards we gain as we do our part. The results are sure, but we must pay the price and take action to merit the success.

Faith Is Truth in Action

Have you ever heard something you felt was true, and it just agreed with you? Then you went one step further and acted on that truth. When we have faith in something, we believe in its truthfulness and that truth motivates us to act to verify our hunch. Our action becomes a response to that truth.

We can look for truth in every aspect of life. When we speak of correct principles, principles of success, or formulas for success, we are speaking of truth. Truth is irrefutable and can be an anchor of strength for us in our lives. We may vary and falter at times in our lives, but truth stays constant. Because of the consistency of truth, we are able to utilize its stability to our benefit. Truth allows us to stay grounded and anchored to our core values even though the world may be changing around us. Learning to take action when truth is learned is wisdom and that wisdom brings about positive change and critical results in our lives.

Truth can be spoken, seen, and heard, and can appeal to our senses and impact our lives in profound ways. To receive truth we must look for it and ponder its meaning. Sometimes we get so busy in our lives that we're oblivious or numb to the truth beckoning us. We must take the time to learn and to put our lives in proper perspective in order to recognize truth.

Do our actions match our core beliefs and values? As we consistently align our lives with truth or correct principles, we place ourselves in a position of power and bring ourselves closer to reaching our potential. Living consistently in this manner allows us to achieve success and brings us peace and happiness. When truth is put into action through faith, it can bring about amazing results and dramatic changes in a person's life. Faith is the driving force of action and is a necessary component to success in every aspect of life.

Faith in Yourself

Having faith in yourself means believing in your ability to take action to meet your goal. Sometimes we doubt ourselves and feel like we are inadequate to meet a difficult challenge, but we have much more strength than we think we do. Instead of dwelling on what you can't do, focus on what you can do. Chances are you are capable of much greater dreams and accomplishments than you think. Believe in yourself and your ability to succeed.

There have been countless times throughout history when oppressed groups of people have fought for their freedom and had faith in their cause. In the American War of Independence from England the colonists were outnumbered, had inferior weapons, were less trained, had less money, and in all aspects were the underdogs, but yet they had faith they could win their freedom. They believed that the ultimate cause of freedom was greater than the loss of their own lives, and their faith and action resulted in the United States of America. Another legendary hero whose faith was instrumental in his cause of freedom was William Wallace. Greatly oppressed by the King of England, Wallace courageously refused to give up on his quest for the liberation of Scotland. Wallace would not accept his hopeless circumstances, but instead relied on his faith, believing he would be victorious until it really was so.

In order to view our potential in life, we need to see through new eyes. By consciously looking at the world differently and training our eyes to see the promise in everything and everyone around us, our clearer vision can transform our lives. People often say, "Take off your rose-colored glasses," meaning that you're seeing the world through a falsely positive light. Well, I disagree. I would much rather be wearing rose-colored glasses than smudged or magnified lenses that would limit my perspective of my remote surroundings or make life seem worse than it really is. Seeing life with a new hope and added perception allows us to view ourselves and others for all that we and they are capable of, focusing on our ultimate potentials. Seeing life and others in this refreshing, new way expands our vision and increases our ability to view the best in others and in ourselves.

I have seen ordinary people do extraordinary things because they had faith in correct principles and accepted the hard, fast truth that they were capable of anything. By gradually visualizing success in all aspects of our lives and applying principles for success to our lives, we will start to look at life with new eyes and at last see our true potential. If we build on correct principles and properly follow natural laws, we literally cannot fail. People become extraordinary because they take responsibility for their choices and decide that no matter the odds or obstacles that stand in their way, they will overcome!

One such ordinary man who produced extraordinary results was Abraham Lincoln. Would you be surprised to know that Lincoln failed on many occasions and suffered greatly with health issues? He lost more than one job during his lifetime, was defeated in several elections, failed in business more than once, lost the love of his life when they were both young, lost his only son as a child, suffered a nervous breakdown, fought depression, had terminal cancer, was born and raised in poverty, struggled with his marriage, and had many people make fun of him throughout his life.

So how did such an ordinary man who suffered so many difficult circumstances become arguably one of the most admired people in the history of his country? What made Lincoln so invincible was his ability to overcome whatever was in front of him—he refused to quit. He had faith in himself and in his ability to succeed, no matter the odds. He recognized that failure is often the price we pay to achieve ultimate success in this life, and he embraced that. The way he responded to his circumstances defined the man he came to be.

We too can overcome anything that stands in the way of success. We may fail at times and get knocked down, but if we get up and persist and believe in ourselves, we can overcome and do extraordinary things. Extraordinary results are gained by ordinary people simply because they refused to quit.

Faith in true principles and in our ability to live those principles unlocks the door to power and astonishing results. We can achieve these personal victories every day. Believe in yourself and live your life according to the potential that lies within you. Decide today that no matter the odds, no matter what stands in your way, that you can take charge of your life and live your dreams.

Value 2: Relationships

Relationships encompass every aspect of life and are critical components to our happiness and well-being. When we connect with others, we feel fulfilled and gain vigor for life as well as a sense of belonging and understanding. The ability or inability to have successful relationships influences our family life, friends, career paths, health, ambitions, dreams, and every aspect of life. Relationships are like water—we cannot survive without them.

Human beings not only need love to survive, but they need to *give* love as well. The main component to any successful relationship is love. When you love someone unconditionally, regardless of that person's weaknesses, and feel that same acceptance and support from that person in return, a true bond grows. This bond can exist in a marriage, in a neighborhood community, and even in a company among coworkers. When you truly value and respect others, you are less critical and more likely to think the best of them—this is what love does for us. It allows us to rise above the superficial and connect with everyone we come in contact with.

Each of us, no matter how independent we are, wants to belong and to be accepted and appreciated by others. You may not realize this, but we all belong to some sort of social unit, whether it be a family, neighborhood, community, club, church, sports team, band, class, or even a country. We all belong to some group, and a great deal of our identity is reflected in how these groups accept us. When we do not feel accepted in our relationships, we will go to extreme measures to fulfill this need. Our need to belong is a driving force of life.

Since November 15, 1994, I've had saved in my files a *USA Today* article about the secret to a long and happy marriage. The article, "Sharing Is the Key Ingredient to a Long-Lasting Marriage," discusses the secrets of success of 576 couples in Long Island, New York, who had been married for more than fifty years. Almost 93 percent of these long-term spouses called their marriages either "very happy" (56 percent) or "happy" (37 percent). These couples also said that the keys to marital longevity were trust (82 percent), a loving relationship (81 percent), and willingness to compromise (80 percent).

Many of these couples also related their personal insights about the success of their marriage. One couple said that the foundation of a marriage is "a four-letter word—love." Another couple cited that the best reason to get married is to learn to grow together. Of the couples, 79 percent attributed the success of their marriages to a good sense of humor, saying that they laugh together every day.

Now, whether you have been married for years or are just coming out of a relationship, I believe we can gain valuable insight from the success of others. Developing meaningful relationships in our lives, whether as a spouse, a parent, or a friend, is an essential element to our overall well-being.

Relationships are vital to our sense of life and purpose. If we are in harmony with those we associate with, relationships can positively influence our lives, allowing us to blossom and feel understood. This understanding validates who we are, enlivens our sense of purpose, and makes us feel important. When we don't feel understood, loved, or needed in a relationship, our sense of self-worth drops, impeding our progress in reaching our goals.

Read between the Lines

Our ability to communicate is essential in building strong relationships with others and is comprised of many aspects, most of which are not even the words you speak. One of my favorite quotes by American philosopher and poet Ralph Waldo Emerson states, "What you are speaks so loudly, I can't hear what you say." Just as Emerson states that an individual's character often speaks louder than words ever could, our nonverbal communication is the same way.

Communication is comprised of both words and nonverbal messages we send to others—eye contact, facial expression, body language, and tone of voice. Think of the different ways we can express the words, "How are you?" By using different tones of voice or different body languages, you can communicate completely contrasting messages even though you're saying the exact same words. In a dull voice you could quickly say, "How are you?" and then look everywhere but the person's eyes. These actions would clearly communicate that you don't really care. On the other hand you might say with concern, "How are you?" as you look the person in the eyes, indicating that you're sincerely interested. Learn to communicate effectively by becoming aware of how you feel. Then communicate those feelings in the way you desire by telling your face, eyes, voice, body language, and attitude to cooperate. If you wish to be successful in any aspect of your life, it's essential that you learn to master interpersonal communication.

Years ago Albert Mehrabian, a professor of psychology at UCLA, conducted a study. In this study he first claimed that there are basically three elements that make up face-to-face communication. Those elements are words, tone of voice, and nonverbal behavior. Second, he concluded that our nonverbal communication is particularly important for expressing feelings and attitudes. Mehrabian's findings, which are quoted and referenced throughout the communication seminar world, are known as the "7%-38%-55% Rule." Simply put, Mehrabian found that in the given circumstances of his study, 7 percent of human communication was the words spoken, 38 percent was tone of voice, and 55 percent was body language. These three components became known as "the three *v*'s of communication": verbal, vocal, and visual.

Even Mehrabian admitted that this ratio of verbal, vocal, and visual communication will not reflect every conversation, but there is overwhelming evidence that nonverbal cues play a key role in how we communicate our thoughts to others. Since Mehrabian's research another study was conducted and printed in the *British Journal of Social and Clinical Psychology* under the title "The Communication of Inferior and Superior Attitudes by Verbal and Non-verbal Signals." These findings showed that all nonverbal cues combined, particularly body posture, had 4.3 times the effect of verbal cues. Regardless which study is more or less accurate, one thing is certain: nonverbal communication is crucial and our ability to communicate is essential to our success.

How effective is the combination of your verbal and nonverbal communication? Do your voice and eyes match your feelings? When you effectively communicate, do you send to others the message you intended? Have you ever felt a certain way but said something totally different? I saw a gentlemen stand up to give a talk one day. He said, "I'm happy to be here today to give this talk," but his voice was monotone, his body was stiff, and his face was expressionless. Who you are and the message you convey are written all over you.

Communication Is a Two-Way Street

Have you ever been around people who talk about themselves so much that you can't get a word in? Effective communication is gauged by how successfully we express our thoughts and feelings, and how effectively we interpret the thoughts and feelings of others. To successfully communicate, we must equally learn to listen. Listening requires an ear and a heart. People may verbally communicate that they are feeling wonderful, but you can tell through their voice and body language that it isn't so. Learn to listen to others by observing their body language and watching for the real message they may or may not be saying. By becoming aware of how you express yourself and learning how to interpret others' words, you will quickly notice your relationships with others becoming stronger.

You've probably heard the saying, "The Lord gave us two ears and one mouth, and so we should listen twice as much as we talk." Listening is an important part of communication and can cohesively bond people to one another. One of my favorite activities is listening to my kids tell me about their day at school. I love to hear about their activities and their feelings and thoughts. We have a very close relationship, and they know I really care.

My wife is an excellent listener and puts me to shame in this quality. She has a way of making a person feel totally understood without saying a word. Sometimes we all just need a sounding board so that we can express our feelings and thoughts. When we are allowed to voice our thoughts, we feel validated and can think more clearly—we feel like we have meaning and importance. Sometimes I'll talk and my wife will sit and listen with her eyes, lean forward, and nod her head. When I'm done, I feel good, like she really understood how I was feeling. Whenever I tell her thanks for helping me sort through my ideas or figure out a solution, she'll laugh and say, "I hardly said anything." Listening with interest helps validate others' importance and crystallizes their thoughts and feelings.

Effective communication can build strong bonds in a relationship and can also have a positive impact on your health. Studies have shown that people are less likely to feel depressed and emotionally distraught when they have someone they can talk to. Look at all the busy psychologists in the world, who get paid to listen to others' problems. When people have someone to listen to, they feel encouraged and loved, and their body and spirit are lifted to a healthier stage.

Our careers are one area in particular that is impacted by communication. If we want to be more in tune with the needs of our company, we must learn how to effectively communicate with our employers and employees. Do you understand what is expected of you at your job? Do your coworkers understand what you expect of them? Major companies lose millions of dollars every year due to poor communication. When we are able to express ourselves effectively and listen intently to the needs of others, we will become more successful at what we do.

Becoming a good communicator and having healthy relationships is essential to success. We must master the art of communication and learn to listen so that we can add value to and gain the rewards of building strong relationships with others. Once we learn to use these skills, they can be of tremendous value to our progress and to the progress of others.

Lose Yourself

We live in a changing world with much complexity and busyness. It's easy to get caught in the thick of thin things, meaning it's easy to spend excessive amounts of time on things of little importance. As we get consumed with endless daily tasks, we enter our own world, sometimes forgetting about the needs of others. We start to think, "I have enough going on myself without having to deal with the problems of others." We talked in chapter 3 about the recipe for success and how universal laws will work for our benefit when we adhere to them. These laws apply to relationships as with any other priority of life: as we lose ourselves in the service of others, we actually find who we really are.

In college I dated a really nice girl, but she greatly misunderstood this natural law as it relates to relationships. One day we happened to be discussing the opportunity to help others, and she exclaimed, "I have so much going on in my life that I don't have time for anyone else's problems." Trying to process her response, I proposed a scenario to her. I said, "What if the person you marry gets in a car accident and can't walk anymore? How would you react?" Her feelings and thoughts came to the forefront when she said, "That would be so tough on me with all the things I couldn't do." She added that she didn't know if she would be able to stay married to him because of the cramp that would put in her lifestyle and all the activities that this would hold her back from. I wondered if she even gave a moment's thought about her hypothetical husband and the devastation that he might feel, suffering complete paralysis. She was so consumed with herself that she could not see the other person's needs. Needless to say, this helped me to see her in a different light and gave me something to reflect on.

When you lose yourself in the needs of another, you discover that your circumstances do not define who you are; rather you are defined by how you respond to your circumstances. Losing yourself empowers you and allows you to take responsibility of something you have direct control over. When you lose yourself in service of others, you are saying that your problems don't control you and that you have power to choose your response and take charge of your life. You begin to recognize that although you have problems, so do others and you can make a difference. As you serve others you will have an increased ability to tackle your own problems and see solutions to your problems, thanks to your new perspective on life.

Problems and adversity will always be present, and all the hours in a day will not alleviate us from these issues. Focusing solely on your own problems will seldom fix them, and the next day you will only be introduced to more problems. Just as we are surrounded by problems, every day we have just as many opportunities to serve others. So give yourself a break from your worries and allow yourself to feel the healing balm that comes from helping someone else. We gain strength as we look beyond ourselves and see the needs of another human being. No matter how tough we feel life is, there is always someone who has it worse. When we look outside ourselves and find the best in others, we also find the best in us. That spark of light becomes brighter when we focus on the needs of others, and this light picks us up and motivates us to be better.

I was raised by wonderful parents, who instilled in me the principle of serving others. My dad was a schoolteacher, so we didn't have a lot, but we had enough. When my siblings and I were just kids, my parents started a Thanksgiving tradition where we would go down to the store as a family and pick out a big turkey, rolls, stuffing, cranberries, and other tasty items to be eaten at a Thanksgiving feast. We would then drive as a family to an area of humble means, where my parents felt like a family could use a little help. We would place the Thanksgiving food items on the porch, ring the doorbell, and run out of sight. As I looked on from a hidden location, I remember seeing the joy of the family receiving this gift and feeling a unique happiness I'd never experienced before.

We can serve in so many ways. Look around and find someone who needs help. This may be visiting a lonely elderly person who has lost her sweetheart, standing up for someone who can't defend himself, holding someone's hand to cross a street, or maybe just listening to someone's tough day. The service we give may be in the form of monetary assistance, but more often than not we donate our valuable time to help someone else. As we forget ourselves in service to others, we will find success in our relationships and a greater strength within ourselves. Forgetting ourselves allows us to find the greater treasure within us.

As we look after the needs of others, we naturally become better at building successful relationships. Those who serve others do not lack problems of their own, but rather they are the ones who understand the formulas for success as they relate to relationships. People who understand this principle find the greatest happiness and success in life. I knew of a man who was a wonderful husband and father. He spent many years of service coaching sports and instilling great integrity and confidence in the young men of his community. He loved to learn and found great joy in the experience of life, and then at a relatively young age he was diagnosed with terminal cancer. When I learned of this my heart sank, and I felt deeply moved for him and his family. Some, when learning of such an event, would stay in bed and throw in the towel. They may give up on their will of life and immerse themselves in self-pity, but not this man. He understood that when you lose yourself in service to others, you find your greatest happiness. The next time I saw him, he didn't say one thing about his diagnosis but instead asked me how life was treating me. He took an interest in everyone around him and didn't spend a moment about his own problems. He was an inspiration to his family and to all those whose lives he influenced for good. To this day, I think of his great understanding of building successful bonds with others—he lived this principle until his last breath of life.

The Worth of Others

Leading up to this chapter we've talked about how capable we are as human beings and how nothing and nobody should hold us back from accomplishing our dreams. We know that our individual potential is limitless, but do we believe others are given this same promise? Do we judge others by who they are instead of by who they can become? Most people overcome great obstacles in life because someone believed in them.

My father was a master at looking for and seeing the best in others, and as a result I saw him inspire many, many people. Have you noticed that others often live up to the reputation we give them, good or bad? When I was a teenager, my father infused so much confidence in me that I never wanted to let him down for anything—most of the time it seemed he thought better of me than I thought of myself. His view of my worth instilled a powerful drive to want to live up to that potential. Although I had my share of follies, my father's wisdom and high expectations helped me avoid many potential pitfalls and dangers. I didn't want to let him down, and that expectation influenced my decisions for good. To this day I'm motivated to live up to the worth my father sees in me, and I've witnessed this same force improve the quality of many lives over the course of my dad's life. We can infuse this same confidence in others if we look for the good in them and see their ultimate worth.

On the contrary I found that my friends with parents who didn't trust them often got in worse trouble, thus living up to the negative reputation their parents labeled them with. When someone believes in us, it makes us more apt to believe in ourselves. As we treat others with respect and see them with the potential they have, they will often fill the shoes of that perception.

Our view of others is reflective of our own biases and judgments, and often reflects how we view ourselves. Do you sometimes feel inadequate and discouraged when someone else succeeds, seeing someone else's accomplishment as a reminder of all the goals you aren't achieving? Sometimes we unintentionally hold others back because of our own perceived limitations. I've seen some great individuals curtail their own success because they allowed others to negatively influence them and fell short of what they could've been. Look for the best in yourself, and it will be easier to see the best in others.

Change Others by Changing Yourself

If you want to change others, begin by working on yourself. Have you noticed that we often point out the faults of another but are unwilling to see our own mistakes? People will not change when we are tearing them down. The best way to motivate transformations in others is to lead by example and improve yourself first.

Many couples wonder why they don't get along or why their spouse never understands their needs. They say that he never listens, she doesn't understand, he is so selfish, she only thinks of herself, he never cleans up after himself, or he doesn't help with the kids. Does any of this sound familiar? We are often too quick to point out the faults of others without looking into our own array of follies. Tearing others down brings resentment, breaks down communication, and causes a spiral of events that leads to misery and unhappiness. Couples forget all too soon the many reasons they married their partner in the first place. They are willing to throw it all away because they feel things would be easier with someone else, but then they get into another relationship and find problems there as well. We will never find a perfect person, and even if we do, would they want to be with us?

Let's face it—we all have plenty to improve about ourselves. Many marriages and relationships could be salvaged if each one of us would focus on improving our own weaknesses instead of spotlighting our partners' failings. Criticizing and demoralizing someone does not reflect the love and concern you have for that person, so turn the mirror around and start with yourself. Work on showing love to your spouse, being more patient with your kids, and communicating your feelings better to your loved ones. Regulate the one person you have control over—yourself. You will be surprised at how much your relationships can improve if you work on this one action.

When you see a positive change in others, reinforce that behavior by recognizing it and complimenting the

improvement. This action works in marriage, with kids, and in any other relationship. When you recognize a good behavior and genuinely compliment the person, they will be likely to do it again. They say to starve the bad behavior and feed the good behavior that you desire, so give less attention to the behavior you don't want and give greater attention to the behavior you do want. I've seen the positive results in my own children with this principle. My little girl would sometimes cry to get her way. I would ignore her whining, and she quickly realized that crying and whining would not get her anywhere. However, when she began to share with her siblings, I would reward her with compliments and sometimes a treat. She is now one of the best sharers I know, and that quality has become a hallmark and strength of her personality.

We may at times feel angry at another's behavior and want to scream, but if we remember that the only person in this life we can control is ourselves, we can train ourselves to focus on the good behaviors in others and work to improve ourselves. As you do these things, your relationships will improve and you will see love return to your home, your marriage, and any relationship you are in. If you have been in a relationship that had an unfortunate ending, start where you are today and go forward. Your life is not about where you have been but where you are today and where you will be tomorrow.

The Gift of Time

The greatest gift you will ever give someone is time. Although it's what most of us yearn for from others, it's also one of the hardest gifts to give. We get so busy in life that it seems easier to help someone through monetary means, but time is cost-free and is usually of greater value.

When I was a young man I spent a couple of years in Puerto Rico doing volunteer work and was impressed by the people's willingness to give of their time so freely to others. They genuinely made me feel like they had all day for me. Sometimes we try to be efficient with people, and it just doesn't work. My wife has reminded me of this on several occasions. I have a tendency to be a checklist guy, and I've realized through my wife's loving nudge that we can be efficient with things but not with people.

My father was a wonderful example of someone who made time for people. As soon as my father returned home from work, he would play sports with my brothers and me. Almost every day of my childhood we would literally play until the sun went down. I have the greatest memories with my father and my siblings as he taught us great principles of life through a love of sports. To this day I enjoy sports, but more importantly I have an incredibly strong relationship with my father. I am sure he could have spent his time doing things for himself, but he chose to give his time to his kids and by so doing created a powerful closeness with us. My father always told me that the best things in life are free, and I now know what he meant—the time we spend cultivating our relationships with those we love is priceless.

Our relationships have a powerful influence on our quality of life. Our ability to connect with people will determine our success in every aspect of life—jobs, health, attitude, families, and much more. We must master the ability to develop a strong and genuine rapport with others. We can improve our relationships by communicating more effectively, losing ourselves in the service of others, seeing others' potential and treating them with respect, helping others improve not by changing them but by changing ourselves, and giving the gift of time. These principles of developing a successful relationship work, and you will see results as you apply them. There are many complexities to human interaction, but as we apply a few simple but powerful principles, we will see positive changes enter every area of our lives. As we have more positive interactions with others, we will catapult ourselves into our full potential and enjoy the success and happiness of deep meaningful relationships.

Value 3: Personal Development

By now you may have noticed that to diversify our lives, we must put faith, others, and our own development first. This is intentional because as we strengthen our faith, put others in highest regard, and discover who we are, we allow ourselves to reach our full potential. Personal development is about improving ourselves and learning how to become the best we can be. Personal development encompasses striving for our greatest dreams, pursuing our life passions, and developing hobbies, talents, and any other attribute that would help us reach our full potential. These three values are interconnected, and therefore each plays a vital role in our overall happiness, success, and well-being.

Personal development is about gaining knowledge and developing ourselves into the best we can be. We all have different interests and desires—this is what makes us unique. For you, personal development might be mastering your attitude, learning to fly fish, attaining a college degree, practicing public speaking, or gaining knowledge through reading and study. Some people love to create and build things. My son is very passionate in this way and often teaches me the principles of mathematical and scientific application in this field. I admire his ambition and interest. Taking time for personal development is essential if we are to reach our potential and maintain a healthy balance in our lives.

Take Time for Yourself

Personal development is a key component to balance in life. We must make personal time a priority or logistically we will never have time to develop in meaningful ways. If we don't make time to develop ourselves, we'll never get a chance to pursue our passions in life and fulfill our dreams. We must diversify our lives enough to give personal development precedence or else we will quickly find ourselves unhappy, stagnant, and useless to others.

Years ago I wanted to pursue a dream of completing a marathon. I was a sprinter in high school but never attempted the long runs, so I knew running a marathon would be a significant enough challenge to really push me and help me achieve something beyond my normal capacity. I trained consistently for several months and was able to tackle that goal and satisfy that dream. Granted, training for the marathon required me to rearrange my schedule a bit to fit in some early morning runs, but because I had planned when I would train, I still was able to meet the other demands and priorities of my life.

Now you may say that you don't have time to train for a marathon or do whatever it is you wish to do. I constantly hear people say, "I never have any time to exercise"; yet those same people seem to find time to play eighteen holes of golf during the day or spend countless hours vegging in front of a television, watching their favorite shows. We find time for those things we truly value. It's not that we don't have the time, it's that we are not willing to spend our time in that way. When we learn to prioritize and balance our lives, we will make time for those things of greatest value.

Balance for Women

Ladies, what is your greatest dream in life? What have you always wanted to do? I'm speaking directly to the women right now because I see many of you who are deprived of time for personal development, and you're suffering because of it. Most women sacrifice much of their own time and talents for the good of their families. This sacrifice is one of the greatest sacrifices one can make, but while family is very important and I would encourage anyone to make great sacrifices in this area, women still need to develop and have an outlet that fosters growth and personal progress. According to the 1997 article "Gender Differences in Depression" published in *Medscape Women's Health* magazine, although depression is a serious illness for both men and women, women suffer from depression approximately 50 percent more than men. Most often this is because women have a greater sensitivity to the needs of others and, as a result, neglect their own personal care. But since personal development is a vital component to a balanced life, we each need to make time for it in order to progress and enjoy the fullness of life.

Women, for your own satisfaction and happiness in life, you must find a balance between helping others and cultivating your own personal growth. I would encourage you to take some time for yourselves, and I encourage the support of your family in this regard. I am not saying to go ballistic and abandon all your current responsibilities, but I am saying that you should make personal development a necessity for your overall well-being. Men seem to find time to golf, have business meetings, lunch appointments, and other activities that stimulate personal growth and development. I find that women often feel guiltier than men about taking time for themselves, but women need personal development just as equally as men do. So, men, please help the women in your lives take the personal time they need so that they can contribute to society and improve themselves too. By consistently bettering ourselves we are more prepared to help others and are more effective in the various roles we have in life. When we are happier, we are more effective. And when we are more effective, we are better spouses, parents, friends, and reach a greater potential in everything in life.

The Learning Sponge

One aspect of personal development is learning. Learning allows us to acquire knowledge, which can give us a stronger sense of self-worth, enable us to have more meaningful interactions with others, and propel us toward attaining our goals. I call personal development "the learning sponge" because life is our opportunity to soak up whatever knowledge we can gain to enhance the quality of each day and reach our ultimate potential.

Learning is the crown jewel of personal development. It is a reservoir of fuel that powers our dreams and makes them reality. Utilize every opportunity to absorb all you can and allow that information to serve you in progressing toward your goals. If you are focused on your goals, your mind will more readily hone in on information that will help you with your needs. As students for life, we are learning and growing as much as we can.

In the wise words of Scottish patriot and hero William Wallace, "Every man dies, but not every man really lives." Each morning the rising sun tells us it's a new day—a fresh canvas on which to experiment and create a masterpiece. Is there an accomplishment on your bucket list that you have always wanted to achieve? Here is your chance to go for it and live your life. Don't settle for mediocrity. Don't be afraid to try because you think you don't know enough or you think you may fail. The only way to "really live" and to really learn is through trial and error.

As you go through life, learning and living, keep a success journal, as I mentioned in chapter 3. Record your feelings, thoughts, events, ideas, and any other useful information that promotes greater success and happiness in your life. Keeping a success journal will help you learn from your mistakes and the mistakes of others so that you can be more effective. As you live, learn, and apply, you can record those experiences from life and gain great strength from these lessons. A success journal is a must for personal development and in achieving a healthy balance to life. A success journal helps us to optimize our learning from life experiences and enables us to reach our greatest potential.

All things can be kept in balance, including personal development, as long as we prioritize wisely. Some people take it too far and neglect their other responsibilities to pursue only personal development. This is called selfishness. We must maintain a healthy balance to life so that we can be fulfilled and have an overall satisfaction in life. Take the opportunity every day to soak up life, learn all you can, and apply that knowledge so that you can explore and achieve your greatest dreams.

Value 4: Health

Health is a major component of balance and success in our lives. I call health a *maintenance priority* because it influences the quality of our lives in every way. Good health allows us vitality to enjoy a potentially longer life with those we love. Good health can significantly enhance our lives, providing us longevity to expand our goals and develop more talents than poor health would allow. No matter how much time or money we have, without good health we will not be able to enjoy our greatest priorities in life. Health can give us the freedom to enjoy life to its fullest and to have the stamina and strength to accomplish our greatest dreams.

In the June 2010 article "How to Live to Be 101" in *Forbes Woman,* centenarians were asked to reveal their secrets of healthy living. Within the research group, one of the key factors of longevity (besides good genes) was a healthy diet that included fruits, vegetables, whole grains, and lean meats (either chicken or fish). Other health factors these centenarians stressed were getting regular exercise, drinking plenty of water, keeping the mind sharp with reading, and enjoying life and good friends. Despite the growing trend to neglect our health, we can rise above the norm and attain a healthy, balanced lifestyle if we're willing to put in the necessary effort.

When we overlook a key component of lifestyle balance, we pay a price just as we would if we didn't properly diversify our monetary assets. Researchers are now calling obesity in America an epidemic. According to the Centers for Disease Control and Prevention (CDC), nearly 34 percent of U.S. adults twenty years and older were obese in 2008, and an estimated 68 percent of U.S. adults are either overweight or obese. This same report also found that childhood obesity in the United States has tripled in the past two decades. The latest CDC estimates indicate that approximately 112,000 deaths per year can be attributed to obesity. Being overweight or obese increases the risk of developing many other diseases such as heart disease, hypertension, stroke, osteoarthritis, diabetes, and much more, and heart disease is actually the leading cause of death in the United States for both men and women. CDC has also found that obesity is a major contributor to type 2 diabetes and that an estimated 70 percent of diabetes risk in the U.S. can be attributed to excess weight. In addition to these findings, *Advertising Age* magazine reported in their February 2008 issue that Americans spent sixty billion dollars on weight-loss products and services in 2009, and CDC estimates that each year Americans spend 148 million dollars in direct and indirect medical costs related to obesity.

Statistically we can see the heavy toll society is paying due to our own negligent health practices. We are cutting our lives short and cheating ourselves dearly of a higher quality of life. Our best option is to decide today to make a change and live the formulas for success as they pertain to health.

No Substitute for Success

Over the years I've known many people who have tried to lose weight using trendy diets, magic pills, and plastic surgery. The bottom line is that these solutions may provide some short-term relief and illusionary results, but they will not give you enduring health to enjoy the greatest quality of life. We can't expect to be healthy if we're maintaining a diet that encourages the consumption of anything we want and promotes a sedentary lifestyle. This formula is faulty, and we would be better off saving our money than buying into these fallacies. There is no quick fix or shortcut to losing weight. There is no shot, pill, diet, or surgery in the world that will successfully substitute the answer for weight loss and good health. There is a price to pay to gain lasting results, and as we follow the laws of health we will gain both the physical freedom and the energy to pursue our goals.

What does it mean to be physically healthy? How do we obtain this energy and vitality? We have already mentioned that the only way we can lose weight is by burning more calories than we eat. Some of you may want to gain healthy weight, so the recipe for this would be to eat more good calories than you burn. Achieving successful results does not need to be complex. Oftentimes we look for answers and pay outlandish amounts of money in search of a quick fix, when the real answers for real results are found in the simple and correct principles that are right in front of us. Recognizing the law is easy, but we must be willing to pay the price. The price as it pertains to health can be found in healthy eating, exercise, sufficient rest, and being responsive to the needs of our bodies and minds. As we comply with these rules we will enjoy an active and healthy lifestyle.

Maintaining a healthy lifestyle brings so many benefits. Besides the obvious physical benefits, a healthy lifestyle refreshes the mind, invigorates the body, and enlivens the soul. When we are physically fit and eating right, we feel better and have more energy; we can do activities with those we love. Being fit gives us freedom, increases our self-esteem, and improves our perception of the world around us. When we are healthy we have a greater potential for longevity and freedom from sickness and disease. Being healthy allows us to soar spiritually and feel connected to a higher source and more able to reach our greatest potential. The mind, body, and spirit are inseparably connected and function best when in harmony with each other. The benefits of being healthy are endless. As we make health a priority in our lives, we will tap into a marvelous source of power and avoid the pitfalls of poor health.

Proper Eating

While growing up, I remember drinking power shakes and eating large amounts of food in an effort to bulk up and gain weight. Being active in sports, my metabolism was on fire, and it seemed my body was a burning furnace that incinerated every calorie I ate. As we get older our metabolisms slow down, and we begin to recognize the need to eat properly and in moderation. The days of eating fast food cheeseburgers for every meal are gone. Still we can afford ourselves some treats and some rewards as we train our bodies and discipline ourselves to eat healthy.

In order to eat the right foods, we must first know what to eat and then discipline ourselves to follow that plan. Everyone's body has individual needs, so I encourage you to research and study what's best for you and then make the necessary diet changes that will lead you to a healthier, happier life. For general guidelines on daily food consumption, I recommend visiting the Web site set up by the United States Department of Agriculture—www.mypyramid.gov. They've categorized the basic food groups as whole grains, vegetables, fruits, milk and low-fat dairy, and meat and beans (consisting of lean meats, poultry, fish, beans, eggs, and nuts). Each of these components, as well as plenty of water, can assist us in gaining the energy and strength we need for good health.

I won't go into an extensive database of foods, but I will mention one vital tip: make sure you read food labels. Be conscious of what you are putting into your body. For example, a diet low in fat and low in sugar is a recommended guideline for healthy living, but be careful that even the low-fat dairy you eat, such as yogurt, does not have an excessive amount of sugar. Some of these labels tout low fat but do not disclose their high amounts of sugar. Be aware of what's in your food to help in your daily eating decisions.

Exercise Model

Exercise is an essential part of a healthy lifestyle and is important for living a longer, healthier, and happier life. From personal experience I know that exercise can reduce stress, help maintain a healthy weight, reduce the risk for chronic disease, and provide a greater sense of overall well-being. Exercise is a well-known way to help control blood pressure; build and maintain bones, muscles, and joints; increase endurance and muscle strength; improve self-esteem; and reduce feelings of depression and anxiety.

On average a person should exercise five times a week for at least thirty minutes each day and should always include exercises that improve cardiovascular, strength and resistance, and flexibility. Cardiovascular activities speed up the heart rate and breathing, and strengthen the heart and lungs. These activities include jogging, swimming, biking, basketball, aerobics, walking, and any other activity that gets the blood pumping. Strength and resistance exercises help build and maintain bones and muscles. These exercises can include weight lifting, push-ups, sit-ups, pull-ups, and any other activity that creates resistance as force is applied. Flexibility is enhanced as we stretch before and after a workout, and do other activities that increase our range of motion. Becoming more flexible will reduce injury and enhance our physical capability. All three of these exercise components are essential in maintaining our health, increasing our physical performance, and maximizing our life experience.

Take Time for Health

Part of a healthy lifestyle is taking time for regular checkups and practicing good personal hygiene. Be in tune with your body's needs and take time to get routine physicals to assess your current health report. These preventive measures can help you avoid more severe health problems that may result from neglect. Personal hygiene is also a component of health and should be observed with proper maintenance of skin, hair, and teeth. Use good judgment in the proper care of these areas.

Our health will greatly impact the quality of life that we enjoy. We must follow the correct principles of health by eating right, exercising, and being vigilant to our physical needs. As we apply this formula we will see positive results and a powerful change come into our lives. When we prioritize health, we amplify our life experiences and enjoy a richness of opportunities. Good health is key to a full life.

Value 5: Resources

As we've discussed many times throughout this book, establishing balance in our lives is critical to our happiness and overall well-being. That balance as it pertains to our finances and our time is no different. The saying that money isn't everything is certainly true, but having no money isn't any fun either. We sometimes hear that money is the root of all evil and that aspiring to be financially sound is wrong. But the truth is, success is not measured in what we have but in who we are. Money in and of itself is not evil; it's what we become or do with our money that determines its value, good or bad. The way we manage our money and time in this life will significantly impact our personal freedoms and our ability to attain many of our goals.

Money can be a valuable resource for us to enjoy a fullness of life. It can provide the time and financial resources to pursue our dreams, allowing us to spend more time doing the things we value most. So what becomes important is the ability to manage our time and resources wisely so that we can effectively and prosperously prioritize our values and pursue our greatest dreams.

Warren Buffet, one of the richest people in the world, put this idea of balance in perspective when he pledged more than 99 percent of his wealth to philanthropy, either during his lifetime or at his death. In June of 2010 *Fortune Magazine* highlighted this philanthropic pledge and recorded Buffet saying, "Measured by dollars, this commitment is large. In a comparative sense, though, many individuals give more to others every day," humbly recognizing countless others who give so much of their resources at a great sacrifice of their own. He continued, saying, "Moreover, this pledge does not leave me contributing the most precious asset, which is time. Many people . . . give extensively of their own time and talents to help others. Gifts of this kind often prove far more valuable than money. A struggling child, befriended and nurtured by a caring mentor, receives a gift whose value far exceeds what can be bestowed by a check."

When it comes to diversifying our lives, I put time and money in the same category because I consider them both necessary resources to attaining an ideal life. If we are barely scraping by financially or are spending all our time attaining wealth, we cannot adequately devote resources to strengthening our faith, building quality relationships, developing our sense of self, and maintaining our health. Health and resources—our two *maintenance values*—allow us to enjoy our most important values in greater abundance and to have the time to do it. Having sufficient financial resources and being wise in their use can provide the time necessary to enjoy life to its fullest and place in highest regard those values that matter most.

We have a great need to diversify our lives just as we do our financial resources. As a financial advisor I would often counsel people to not put all their eggs in one basket, but to instead diversify their monies into different investment vehicles and companies. That way if one investment went bad my client wouldn't lose everything. The wisdom to invest in such a way allows us to stay balanced and manage our funds according to our individual needs. We must learn to balance our time and efforts in the same way so that all our energy doesn't go to one or two sole values in our lives while abandoning the others.

Who's the Boss?

There was a certain man whose money I managed for years. He had become extremely wealthy in his occupation and through his investments. He had a mansion and much acreage with incredible amenities. He had maids, fancy cars, and recreational facilities that rivaled some amusement parks. He was a hard worker and spent fourteen hours a day maintaining a livelihood he had established for his family. He took great pride in what he had achieved and was no doubt a wealthy man as it pertained to financial resources.

One day as I was visiting with this man, I asked him if he had everything in life that he wanted. He paused for a moment and said, "I wish I had more time. More time with my family, more time doing things that I am passionate about, more time to enjoy life." Here was a man that most people envied because of his financial wealth, yet he felt he was a slave to his possessions and had to keep earning enough money to maintain that lifestyle. This man was not free but rather at the mercy of his empire. He was very good at making money, but he was not so good at its management. He didn't know how to tap into the freedoms money could provide. He became consumed with the things money could buy and neglected the greater values that money couldn't afford. He missed his kids' childhood—years that could never be duplicated—and then spent the rest of his life trying to catch up.

A few years later this man sold his company, his mansion, and many of his possessions, and moved into a home with less upkeep. In the process he discovered real treasure in his newfound family time, realizing he had much more freedom by properly managing his money and time. He was no longer a slave to his empire, having to beckon to its every crisis. His simpler life provided him with more happiness and freedom than he had ever experienced. He discovered true wealth and, to this day, spends much of his time with his kids and grandkids, enjoying the treasures of life.

Work Hard and Work Smart

What are your financial goals? What is it that wakes you up in the morning and gets you to work? Is it to pay the bills? Is it to buy that long-awaited first home? Is it to take that dream vacation or spend more time with your family? Our time is a precious commodity, and therefore whatever our work or current project, it deserves the focus required to maximize our efforts. Make your work time most effective so that you can then spend the rest of your day doing what you really are passionate about.

Some people can accomplish in four hours, what others may need eight to ten hours to do. Your ability to focus and manage your time will make you more proficient and better able to reach your aspirations in the timeliest manner. There are only twenty-four hours in a day so make your time count. Minutes of your life become your days, weeks, months, years, and your lifetime. We must manage our time so that life does not pass us by, leaving us wondering where it all went. According to New York Yankees manager and Baseball Hall of Famer Casey Stengel, "There are three kinds of people: those who make things happen, those who watch things happen, and those who ask, 'What happened?'"

Making things happen requires us to take responsibility for our time and utilize our resources wisely. I remember spending some years in real estate. Real estate is a very social profession with many activities that can occupy your time if you let them. There are sales meetings and sales tours, then sales lunches and sales training. People can get so caught up in the activities that they don't spend their time actually working and making money. In order to see results in what we do in life, we must spend more time in the doing and less time in the talking and watching. When we work hard and work smart we will see results and get closer to our ultimate goals in life.

The real measure of one's effectiveness is by the results they bring. We all have been around people who spend a lot of time doing nothing. They are busy but not effective. There was a man in a sales company whose boss asked him how his day went. The man replied, "I was so busy today. I drove the company car more than two hundred miles, over hills and valleys. I saw thousands of people walking on the streets and had a great lunch and talked business with the waitress." The boss said, "So you didn't sell anything, huh?" The man replied, "No," and the boss said, "You're fired."

We can spend time being busy but not accomplish a thing. We must have a sense of purpose to what we do so that our time is well spent in gaining results. Being effective is measured in results. We must not confuse being busy with being effective. Being effective with our time will allow us to gain the results we are looking for. Focus your energies toward obtaining your goal and spend your time wisely.

Money Matters

During my career as an investor I had the opportunity to work closely with people from varying income levels who had different objectives as to how they would use their monetary resources. I saw individuals who had amassed great wealth, noting both the opportunities and the hurdles that come with that package. Many used their resources to establish a life of service and gave greatly of their time for the benefit of others. I worked with some families who squandered their fortunes, spending a lifetime consumed with material goods. I also worked with some who struggled to make ends meet to support their families. This financial despair greatly impacted their lives and was a point of great pain and disappointment.

Money can have an enormous impact on our lives, often being either the means to pursue our five core values or the massive hurdle keeping us from our dreams. Each of us views money in different ways, but we all need it to live. Money can be used for the good of man and can be the means of providing us with the time and resources to enjoy those things and people we value most. Money in and of itself is not the real value but rather what it can provide. The peace, security, and time that financial resources give us can be of great value and greatly impact our quality of life and the pursuit of our greatest dreams.

Common Denominators for Success

Those who say that money doesn't matter apparently don't see that 80 percent of all divorces are caused by financial difficulties, according to an American Bar Association survey. Now, this is not to say that we cannot be happy on very little money, because we can, but it is to say that a lack of money can cause distress and tension in our lives. One of my greatest memories was graduating from college and moving to Oregon with my wife. We were dirt poor, as most college students are, but found a little apartment in Tigard, Oregon. We had one car and both of us were working to get ahead. When we went out for our weekend date night, we would go to Chili's to buy chips and salsa, and ask for two waters. We felt like we were living the high life. Those were some of our funniest memories. However I think we all would agree that we would rather have the peace and security of financial stability than the stress of penny-pinching and financial instability. Money does matter, and how we manage it greatly impacts our lives and is a key component to a balanced and successful life.

Financial Rule of Thumb

There is nothing wrong with having aspirations of financial freedom. Financial freedom can be the means of unlocking the door to more time to pursue those values that are of greatest importance to you. No matter what economic condition you are currently in, here is the time-tested magical formula for financial security: spend less money than you make. There it is. Not so magical, is it? While this may seem obvious, you would be surprised at how few follow this rule. I have known people who have great jobs and produce a healthy income, and yet they spend more than they make because of a costly lifestyle. Then I know others who have a very average income but spend much less than they make and have great financial security.

Looks can often be deceiving. We may see someone who lives in a mansion and drives incredibly expensive cars but has a ridiculous amount of debt. When people begin to make more money, oftentimes they increase their lifestyle to match their increased pay. Many wonder why they are never able to get ahead when they are making so much more than they used to. Others may live a much simpler life and yet have reservoirs of financial resources. We can't judge others' circumstances on face value. There is nothing wrong with having those things in life you want, but there is wisdom in living within your means and spending less than you make. The ability to manage your money and live within your means is an important skill that will provide you the peace and security you need to achieve this desired balance.

In life we often have a tendency to want to keep up with others, particularly when it comes to material possessions. We compare what we have (or don't have) to what we perceive others have and end up buying things just to keep up an appearance. Usually this type of comparison leads to bad financial decisions and a waste of time and energy. Keep your own pace, and stay within your comfort zone of what suits your family's and your individual needs. Spend your time wisely, managing your own financial resources to attain your dreams and less on what others are doing or else you will quickly lose focus of what you're working for.

Living within your means and exercising good financial decisions can unlock the door to peace, stability, and resources to achieve your dreams and maintain a healthy balance to life.

Money does matter, but it's the value we place on that money and what we do with those resources that matter most. The greatest value of money is time. Time allows us to focus on what matters most. Time can provide us greater opportunities to learn, grow, and pursue our dreams and greatest priorities of life. As we manage our resources wisely, we will discover our greatest reward, and that is the value of time.

The Value of Time

When we finish our journey of life, what will people remember most about you? The amount of money you made will hold very little significance, but how you spent your time will be the lasting memory left to others. What impact in life did you create with your time? Was your time spent primarily on yourself or in service to others? The greatest men and women in my life who have passed on spent their time helping others and doing things that contributed to society. They were icons of faith who applied correct principles to every aspect of their lives and spent their personal development time improving themselves so that they could add greater value to the lives of others.

One of the greatest values of time is the ability to experience life at its fullest. My greatest memories are moments spent with my family and loved ones—the times that I've held my beautiful children in my arms or told them stories at night or played hide-and-go-seek with them. Some of the most wonderful time spent with my wife has come as we've talked about our plans for the future and just enjoyed each other's companionship. Time allows us to experience these priceless moments of life that add significant value to our existence.

In August 2009 one of my older brothers and I had a chance to spend some time together on a fishing adventure in the Canadian wilderness. We spent one full week hauling in more than a hundred lake trout, some being over thirty pounds. We had such a great time, I hung a picture of this adventure in my home office. This plaque reminds me of the importance and value of time. Fill your life with memories created through the application of true principles—principles that allow you the time to live your dreams and enjoy life's greatest moments.

We are managers of our own time, and because time is of such great value, we must be efficient in its use. Take out a piece of paper and map out how you will use your time on a daily, weekly, monthly, and annual basis to achieve your lifelong goals and dreams. Make sure that every day you are making progress to achieve these pursuits. When we fail to plan our time, we plan to fail. How many of us say, "You know, I really would love to . . ." but never do anything about it. We must take charge and responsibility for our time. If we don't, we will utter, like many do in the twilight of their years, "I wish I would have . . ." Live your life and plan your time so that you have no regrets.

Don't Get Caught in the Thick of Thin Things

Time is precious so don't get caught wasting it on meaningless events. Some time must be spent fulfilling responsibilities, but in reality we waste a lot of time doing things that don't matter. For example, we spend a great deal of time worrying about things that are out of our control. This time spent meaninglessly could be used for more effective gain. Spend less time gossiping, bickering, and wasting negative energy on things that have no value. We can gain those minutes and hours back by eliminating those time-wasting tasks that do not get us closer to our goals. As you make more positive use of your time, you will see the difference it makes in your life.

Spend your time building up, not tearing down. Be a catalyst in someone's progress, not an anchor to hold him or her back. Spend your time being positive about life, not negative. Spend your time focusing on the good in others, not the bad. Spend your time saying, "I'm sorry," "Thank you," or "I love you," not allowing your pride or procrastination to stand in the way of your relationships. Cut out the trivial, meaningless, and negative trash of life, and spend your time making the world a better place. How you spend your time is up to you, so spend it wisely and spend it in a positive and meaningful way. This wise use of your time will make you a better, more effective person and will maximize your time on values that matter most.

Determine a schedule that is built around your values and maintains a healthy balance. Some people claim they don't have time to work out, yet they find time to golf, shop, and do other things that have less value. We make time for those things that matter most to us. I am entirely convinced that if we determine to live a healthy, successful, and balanced life, we will find time to prioritize our values. Sit down once a week and map out your days. What time will you wake up? When will you work out, leave for work, and go to bed? Some things will come up that you don't expect. Roll with the punches and don't get flustered, but get back on track and back to your schedule. Review your schedule every morning and at the conclusion of every week. Schedule time for unforeseen events such as helping the kids with homework, taking time for a friend who needs a listening ear, and other events that require extra time. We can't always account for everything, but a plan will steer us in the right direction and keep us on track to achieve our goals.

Take a personal inventory every night and evaluate how your time was spent. Within which of the five values—faith, relationships, personal development, health, and resources—could you have been more effective? Where was time spent that was most meaningful to you? Evaluating the use of our time and learning from where we spend it will help us become more effective in life.

Take Time to Smell the Roses

As you pursue a healthy balance to life, make sure you take time to smell the roses. Some of your greatest moments will come during the quiet times as you contemplate what matters most. Life is meant to be enjoyed, so don't get so caught up in your schedule that you lose sight of the very purpose for which you are trying to be effective. As you come to better understand that happiness in based on consistent application of correct principles, you will discover a freedom and zest for life that will be unquenchable. You will have a drive, determination, and vigor for life that will change the way you see the world. Enjoy the journey of life. You will have roadblocks and various obstacles that will come in your path, but as you view these challenges as opportunities to grow, you will gain new perspective and enthusiasm in pursuing your dreams. Pause long enough to enjoy others without having an agenda and appreciate the journey of life and all its beauties.

It is in these moments that we make lasting memories and realize the true value of life.

Our life is made up of time and our results will be measured by what we have done with that time. Use your time wisely and spend your time in the values of greatest importance. Write down the dreams you want to accomplish, and then plan out your days, weeks, months, and years, to reflect the importance of those values. Find time for those things that matter most and then spend your time doing them. As we manage our time wisely we will see results in our lives, and we will receive a sense of peace and satisfaction.

Effectively managing our time and money will make an unbelievable difference in our quality of life. Our ability to properly manage these resources adds value to everything we do and enables us to reach our potential to live a healthy and balanced life. Investing our money and time wisely will open doors and unlock opportunities that will allow us to put in first regard that which matters most and pursue our greatest dreams.

Recap: Balance Your Life

Keeping our lives balanced is essential to finding happiness and peace, and reaching our potential in life. Just as a recap, each one of us has five core values in life—our critical values being faith, relationships, and personal development, and our maintenance values being health and resources (time and money). Each of these values serves a purpose and enhances our quality of life. We must spend time making these values a priority in our lives.

When we neglect any one of these five core values, we suffer the consequences and create a void in our lives. This void, when not cared for, becomes like a domino effect, infiltrating all other aspects of our lives. If four of our core values are going well, but we are deficient in one, the other four areas will eventually feel the negative effects and suffer. True success comes from the consistent application of correct principles in every aspect of our lives. Our ability to keep this balance will determine the ultimate success we achieve and influence our ability to reach our potential and live our dreams.

Being balanced means consistently applying correct principles to every aspect of life; without balance there is no way to enjoy total fulfillment and total success. I believe that the leading cause of human deficiency is that we simply are not applying this principle. That is to say, I think our inability to live a balanced life has much to do with sickness, both emotionally and physically. We often get so wrapped up in one or a few core values of life that we leave ourselves totally deficient in the values that directly affect our happiness and overall sense of well-being.

As we maintain a healthy balance to life and apply correct principles of success in each aspect of life, we will have a much smoother ride and be able to enjoy fullness in our capacity of life. Our ability to establish and achieve this balance will propel us to reach our greatest potential and allow us to live life to its fullest.

Formula 6:
In the Zone

Focus is achieved as we overcome roadblocks to success.

Limitation Barriers

My definition of a limitation barrier is anything that alters our focus, taking us out of the zone, and impedes us from achieving our goals. In prior chapters we've discussed how ultimately the only limitations in life are those we place upon ourselves. We have power within us to overcome anything that blocks our path. Therefore financial setbacks, lack of opportunity, or insufficient motivation may appear to be limitation barriers, but really we are the ones stopping ourselves from living our dreams.

In order to achieve our greatest potential we must learn to overcome limitation barriers. These roadblocks to success could be fear, doubt, excuses, negative labels, guilt, pain, procrastination, and other paralyzing obstacles. When we allow these hurdles to divert our attention, we often lose focus, momentum, and time, suspending us from taking necessary action to obtain that goal.

Take a look at your life and see what it is that stands in your way. Most of us want so much more out of life, but we give up on the dreams, feeling it impossible to achieve such heights. Winston Churchill once said, "A pessimist sees the difficulty in every opportunity. An optimist sees the opportunity in every difficulty." Success is not the absence of obstacles, but rather it is our ability to overcome those barriers that stand in our way of greatness. It's all in our attitude and point of view. We must dispel all of the myths and roadblocks that limit our ability to achieve our dreams. Change your way of looking at life and realize that you cannot wait to go after your dreams until the path is free of diversions—such a path doesn't exist. Some of the greatest men and women in history have overcome great difficulties and trials to achieve excellence and realize their dream.

Stevie Wonder is one of the greatest musicians and songwriters of all time. Blind since birth, Wonder overcame many obstacles in his life to achieve his dreams. Many people doubted his ability to succeed in music due to his lack of vision. But Stevie Wonder saw things with a different perspective. He said, "Just because a man lacks his eyes, doesn't mean he lacks vision." Wonder did not let anything, including blindness, stand in his way of achieving twenty-one Grammy Awards, recording more than a handful of No. 1 hits and becoming the youngest recipient ever to receive a lifetime contribution to arts and culture at the Kennedy Center. Here is a man who didn't give in to many legitimate excuses for not achieving his dreams. Instead he stayed focused on his goal and could not be detoured by any obstacle.

There are countless other everyday heroes who have overcome great obstacles of life to achieve victory. Take for instance Bethany Hamilton, an American surfer who survived a horrific shark attack in which she lost her arm. With determination and much physical therapy, she courageously returned to surfing. Or how about Stephanie Nielson? She was a young mother of four who suffered burns over 80 percent of her body after surviving a plane crash in the desert of southern Arizona. Her heroic recovery and attitude of hope and faith have touched thousands of people worldwide. Or Viktor Frankl, an Austrian neurologist who saw his family murdered, endured incredible personal torture, survived the Holocaust, and became an inspiration to the world. Each of these heroes, while facing unimaginable circumstances, responded resiliently and chose to focus on what they could do. They overcame amazing odds and triumphantly have become sources of strength, hope, and inspiration to us all.

Stevie Wonder, Bethany Hamilton, Stephanie Nielson, Viktor Frankl, and many other powerful individuals saw their difficulties as opportunities; and instead of letting those trials defeat them, they took their circumstances as challenges to rise above and have now become inspirations to us all. We all face difficulties in our life. These trials may not come in the way of blindness or severe injury, but they can be every bit as debilitating. These difficulties may be depression or fear or tremendous self-doubt. Whatever your limitation barrier, you can overcome it.

Fear

Years ago I knew a man who became paralyzed by his fears. He had led a successful life and had done quite well for himself financially. His family was wonderful, and he was a man of great faith, but he ended up making some poor financial decisions and, as a result, became paralyzed with fear. This fear occupied his mind and literally stopped him in his tracks. This once charismatic, confident, accomplished man had lost sight of who he was and stopped believing in his true capabilities. He went from being very active to sitting at home and wallowing in his misery and complaining about his "lost time," as he described it. He said that he had thrown everything away—all that he'd worked for—and had let down his entire family. He was terrified that he could never succeed again, and as a result of his loss of confidence, he no longer knew how to strengthen and encourage others. His fear had become insurmountable.

One day I had an opportunity to talk to this man at length. I'd watched him struggle for some time, so I asked him what his plans were. He said, "I don't know. I've lost everything." I pointed out to him that he had not lost everything. Financially he'd had a major set back, but he remained one of the wealthiest individuals I had ever met. He had a beautiful family with children who admired and respected him for his values and the incredible example he had been to them growing up. He had a supportive wife who loved him and had great confidence in him. He believed in living correct principles and had enormous faith in God. He was physically strong and free from sickness and disease. He had great dreams and plans for his life, many of which he had already been able to

Common Denominators for Success

fulfill and enjoy. After talking for hours, he realized that some poor investment decisions had temporarily caused a financial void but that his true wealth was still intact. He regained his strength and vigor for life, and continued his lifelong pursuit of accomplishing his dreams. He eventually succeeded in providing once again for his family, and he overcame his fear by deciding to take action and work within his circle of influence to overcome his temporary setbacks.

Fear can paralyze us at times. The interesting characteristic of fear is that this negative feeling keeps us from acting when we need action the most. When a person is in cold temperatures and stops moving, he's dead. Fear has the same effect on our dreams, killing them the instant we lose momentum and start to drag. Recognizing fear as an obstacle that suspends action can help us move past this speed bump. Acting even in the face of adversity will punch fear square in the mouth and stunt its ability to distract us. Fear in and of itself provides no necessary value unless it serves to protect us from harm. For example, being afraid to jump off a cliff is a good fear that paralyzes action. This paralysis keeps us safe and alive; however, unnecessary fear that prevents us from accomplishing our dreams is of no value and only detracts from our purpose. Learn to recognize fear and take action to overcome it before it consumes you.

Doubt Nothing

We all have a tendency to doubt our abilities sometimes. Doubt, much like fear, suspends our action toward achieving a goal because it convinces us that we're foolish and that our dreams are not possible after all. When we believe something is possible, we naturally take the action necessary to achieve our objective. When we doubt something, we begin a self-fulfilling prophecy of not achieving it and cite countless reasons why it was not possible. The truth is that we limit our dreams and capabilities because of our own doubt.

So once we've recognized that doubt is standing in our way, what do we do? The next step is to determine the source of the negative influence. If we have doubt we are either perpetuating that doubt within ourselves or surrounding ourselves with negative influences that curtail our confidence. Identify where these influences of doubt originate and determine a course of action to minimize the collateral damage.

If the negativity and doubt originate in ourselves, we must replace them with positive affirmations and self-imaging. While this may sound simple, it requires self-discipline and determination. The good news is that it can and will effectively change the way you view yourself and the world around you. Don't worry if this exercise seems a little uncomfortable at first. Sometimes it takes a little effort to break old habits, but once we start to see the positive effects of the new routine, we gain enough confidence to make the change permanent. When a negative thought runs through your mind, make a conscious decision to replace it with a positive one. Your thoughts greatly influence your actions and have an enormous effect on your ability to break through and reach your potential.

For example, let's say that you're giving a speech in front of a classroom. Fear and doubt begin to set in as you wonder if you can do this. You feel like you'll fail and that everyone will be an eye witness to your embarrassment. Stop this talk right there. Tell yourself instead that you can do it. Say that you will be successful in delivering your speech, and in fact, you are going to have fun giving it. And if you happen to make a mistake, you will laugh realizing that it's no big deal. How we view our situation becomes our reality, and if we successfully isolate our negative thoughts and replace them with encouragement, we can overcome doubt and fear.

Sometimes doubts about ourselves are derived from the opinions of others. People around us can influence what we think about ourselves because we give value to their words—we empower them to influence us for good or for bad. When we open ourselves up to others' scrutiny, our emotions are then susceptible and likely to fluctuate solely upon the waves of others' inconsistent and temperamental opinions. Sometimes when people are unhappy, they want others to be miserable as well, so they purposefully tear us down to make themselves feel powerful. Their negative opinions oftentimes have nothing to do with us and have everything to do with their own insecurities. Despite the inconsistencies of others, we can maintain a positive and constant outlook on our ability to succeed.

Eliminate doubt by surrounding yourself with positive people who have your best interest in mind. As we learn to take charge of our own thoughts and surround ourselves with positive influences in and outside of ourselves, we will begin to eliminate doubt and achieve a healthy confidence. As we take responsibility for our own lives and our own thoughts, we will overcome unnecessary doubt that would impede our progression.

Excuses

Years ago my kids and I created an acronym for Anderson, our last name. Within each of the letters are statements that we try to adhere to as a family and that help us elevate our commitment to excellence. This acronym now hangs on a plaque in my office, and the "N" in Anderson reads, "Never complain, blame, or make excuses." My kids know that I cannot stand excuses. When we make excuses we neglect or rationalize our lack of responsibility. We come up with reasons we did not succeed. Now, I do know there are valid excuses at times in our lives that are beyond our control. If we are late for a dinner appointment because our car breaks down, there is very little we can do about it; however, the excuses I speak of are the ones we do have control over but fail to take responsibility for. You know the difference.

The excuses that limit our actions become the seeds of failure. As we blame external reasons for our lack of performance, we gradually adjust to that mentality and begin to look for external excuses for our laziness or poor planning. I once worked with an individual who blamed everyone and everything for his lack of results. When he didn't complete a task it was either that someone didn't explain it well enough or that he didn't have the resources to accomplish the task. Excuses plagued his performance, and he excused his way out of a job. When we make excuses we give ourselves permission to fail. We allow ourselves to get off the hook and merit a reason for a poor performance. I am always refreshed when I find someone, who even in failure, will take responsibility rather than make up an excuse. We all fall short of the mark at times, but we must take ownership of our lives.

Expect great things of yourself and commit your life to excellence. As we accept responsibility for our choices, we take ownership of the life we've created. Think of the great men and women who have overcome nearly impossible odds to accomplish a life of greatness. Instead of floundering for excuses of why they could not, they came up with reasons why they could. I am sure that Stevie Wonder could've come up with plenty of justifiable excuses for why he couldn't succeed, but instead he thought of reasons to succeed and refused to let his unique circumstances become excuses. Throughout our lives we too overcome seemingly insurmountable odds to succeed and to achieve results.

This same principle of taking responsibility for our actions applies to relationships. Years ago a good friend of mine was having some struggles in his marriage. He had made some mistakes but deeply loved his family. He struggled to forgive himself and felt guilty about some of the things he had done because he knew he had been the cause of some deep emotional pain to his family. Although he had been knocked down, he did not want to lose his family and decided to fight for them. He turned his life around and reestablished wonderful and strong relationships with his wife and children. He not only took ownership for his mistakes but also realized he could change and become the man he always intended to be. With a loving and supportive wife by his side, he dusted himself off and reclaimed his beautiful family and his lease on life. He overcame his discouragement and applied the one thing he had in his control—his future actions.

We all make mistakes in this world. We all suffer failures in relationships, personal goals, health, finances, and other areas of our life at times. But we never fail unless we fail to take responsibility for our actions. There is hope knowing that no one is perfect, but as we perfectly keep trying to better ourselves and not make excuses, we will gain wisdom, respect, and determination to reach our goals.

Look Forward

Another roadblock that sometimes creates a barrier to our success is past failures. We all make mistakes in life and fall down from time to time. Success is not the absence of those times we stumble—the most successful people fail and fail often, but they don't stay down.

American football coach Vince Lombardi is known for saying, "Quitters never win, and winners never quit." I've always admired the athlete who fails but then rises to the occasion to find victory again. Brett Favre, the famous Green Bay Packers quarterback, would sometimes throw three or four interceptions in a single game and still come back to put together a winning drive to claim victory. After throwing an interception, most quarterbacks would feel discouraged and be hesitant to keep throwing the ball for fear of another failure. Not Brett. He would throw time and time again with the same tenacity as the one before. He recognized that he was human and would make mistakes, but he would keep getting up until he succeeded.

I know many people who live in the past. They dwell on moments when people have offended them or circumstances that dealt them a poor hand. They carry around bitterness for others and begin to distrust everyone, determining that they must look out only for themselves. They harbor grudges, feel victimized, and give up on the good in the world. These people live so much in the past that they completely miss all the opportunities that are in front of them that could uplift their life. They are so wrapped up in things that are beyond their control that they completely stop forward progress. They cannot look past the situation and become obsessed, miserable,

Common Denominators for Success

and unhappy. This is no way to live. It is completely ineffective and will lead nowhere but to sorrow and pain.

How tough would it be to drive a car looking backward? Would we see the signs in front of us? Would we miss our turn or know how many miles it is to Topeka? When we live life looking through our rearview mirror, we miss great opportunities for happiness and personal development. For the most part there is little we can do to change the past. Instead put the past in perspective and learn from it; visualize the future ahead and prepare for it; and focus on the present and live it!

Learning from the past means taking an active role in preparing for the future. All of us have had disagreements with people we love and wished we could hit rewind and erase our words or actions. Oftentimes we dwell on past conversations or circumstances that we have no control over. When we belabor a situation that is already in the past, we preoccupy our minds with things that we can't change. What's done is done, and the only thing we can do now is continue forward, taking responsibility for our actions, seeking to make amends, and being more determined to be smarter next time. After a disagreement we may wish to apologize to our friend or bring our sweetheart flowers or make some positive gesture to help remedy the situation. These are all good things to bring peace and trust back into a relationship, but don't waste your energy reliving events from the past that you cannot change. Instead spend your time proactively changing your circumstances for the better. Let the past give you the opportunity to learn and change so that you are better prepared for the future.

Learn to let things go. Learn to forgive others. When we refuse to forgive someone of a trespass against us, that resentment spreads within us like a harmful poison. When we forgive we release that destructive poison and allow ourselves to move forward in a positive direction. Even if we harbor anger against someone, the last thing we want to do is let that person control our lives even more by wasting energy and time dwelling on what they did. Let that stuff go, learn to forgive, and move forward with your own progress. This also allows others to move forward as well. We all make mistakes, and we all stand in need of even second and third chances at times.

Recently I read a touching story about a woman from Kansas named Sue whose elderly father was murdered in his home. The crime yielded the assailant less than twenty dollars and an old truck. Sue commented that when she went to the trial of the man who had committed this crime, everyone in the courtroom was filled with hatred and they expected her to harbor similar emotions.

Instead of letting anger consume her, Sue decided on another plan. Although this crime was horrific and very painful, she realized that holding onto anger would not bring her father back. In fact, that anger would ultimately destroy her too if she let it. She chose to take the higher road. When Sue received permission to visit the man who had killed her father, she courageously told the man that she forgave him for what he had done. The man couldn't understand how she could do that. Sue said, "I didn't think of him as a killer, I thought of him as a human being."

This heartfelt story of forgiveness influenced countless people, and Sue became friends with this man until the day of his execution. Her willingness to forgive touched the lives of many, including the assailant, who became a devout Christian before he was executed. Sue refused to dwell on the past, but she instead made the best of her circumstances and turned a terrible situation into one of hope and inspiration.

We cannot control others. We can't control if someone says or does something hurtful—the only person we can control is ourselves. We have to choose our response every day in every moment, deciding to either dwell on a situation or move forward. When we dwell in the past we become rooted there, replaying conversations or events over and over again until they poison us. Dwelling on the past wastes energy that we could have used to accomplish our goals and live our dreams, so choose to do something productive, something within your control. You are the author of your life and the only one who determines your choices.

As we learn to look forward instead of backward, we will train ourselves to not be afraid of making mistakes. We will recognize that our mistakes are ultimately what will teach us how to reach our goals. And as we learn to keep looking forward despite our failures, we will be better and better prepared to reach new goals in the future.

Be 100 Percent in the Moment

Distractions not only cause us to dwell in the past, they can also keep us from the living in the present. We must be 100 percent in the moment at that time to be effective. Rather than mull over tomorrow's to-do list, focus on what you are doing right now and be completely in the zone. Clear your mind of unnecessary worries and focus on being the best at what you have control over in that moment. That other stuff will wait for you tomorrow. The moment you have before you may not.

This focus of energy can also be applied to relationships. When you're talking to your spouse, visiting with a friend, or enjoying a lunch break with a coworker, you can be 100 percent there in that moment. So instead of thinking what you're going to say next during a conversation, listen to what is being said. When you are there—mind, body, and spirit—in that moment, you are able to clear your mind and give your undivided attention to the person you are with. Others will greatly appreciate this effort, and you will be much more effective in your communications and in all your relationships.

I remember spending countless hours negotiating real estate. For years I would talk for more than ten thousand minutes each month on my cell phone. I calculated my time on the phone to be about one third of my life during those years, including the hours I was asleep. I realized that my life was too hectic and that I was not taking as much time for the things that mattered most. I would come home from work and be there physically but not mentally. Oftentimes I would still be thinking about the next deal and everything I had to get done the next day. My family time wasn't as fulfilling during that time, because I was no longer living in the present. One day it hit me that I would never have that time with my kids again. I learned a great lesson about giving precedence to what I valued most and living in the moment. By doing this I was a more effective father and had a much more enjoyable time. Sure enough, my work waited for me until the next day, and my mind was fresher for it. Now I rarely take a call after five or six o'clock because I'm enjoying my family. That time is precious to me, and I don't want to miss it.

Being 100 percent in the moment can also help you pursue excellence and achieve your personal dreams. Whether you want to compete in a triathlon, write a book, or invent something, you can focus 100 percent in that moment to accomplish that task. In fact, it becomes critical to focus on what it is that you really want so that your time can be most effective. You will be so surprised what you can actually accomplish when you get rid of the junk in your life.

In order to be in the zone and keep our eye on the desired end result, we must surround ourselves with constant reminders of what is of greatest value. In my office, I am surrounded by those values that encompass my life. Symbols of faith, family, personal pursuits, health, and resources are represented. On my walls I have a portrait of George Washington kneeling in prayer by his horse at Valley Forge and an image of the Founding Fathers signing the Declaration of Independence. These images represent truth and remind me of the faith I am seeking to have. They motivate me to similarly apply correct principles of faith in my life.

In another corner of my office is a picture of my family, representing relationships in my life that are of greatest value. Hung nearby is a plaque, which I've mentioned before, with the name ANDERSON inscribed. This plaque displays the acronym that my son and I created, with each letter of our last name representing a characteristic or value to emulate as a family. Each one of my kids knows what the letters represent and tries to honor those expectations.

In the same room I also have images and objects that remind me of my personal goals and passions, inspire me to prioritize health, and motivate me to use wise discretion of my time and resources. Some of these images embody my sports interests, such as running a marathon, and my hobbies, such as fishing, which are represented in plaques displayed in my office. Other interests I have are reflected in great quotes, sayings, and stories that symbolize the importance I place on attitude. Each of these reminders serves as a motivator of personal development, accomplishments, and desires that I consider to be of tremendous value. Each of us has a different bucket list of personal achievements and dreams we wish to accomplish and experience. Surround yourself with those reminders that will motivate you to be your best and reach your potential.

Recap: Stay Focused on the Prize

A vital weapon in overcoming roadblocks to success and living in the moment is our ability to focus. We are most effective when we are attentive to the task at hand, positively directing our thoughts, words, actions, and energies to that which we want to accomplish. So, for example, if you want to improve your relationship with your spouse, focus on how you can better yourself, not on how your spouse needs to change. When we learn to direct our attention and energies to being our best at what we are doing in that moment, we increase our chances for success.

As we pursue our dreams in life, we will be challenged with roadblocks to success. These obstacles will attempt to knock us off course and distract us from our plan of action. When we allow these speed bumps to suspend, delay, or eliminate our ability to take action toward our goal, we start to lose focus, and we begin to settle for a life of complacency and being less than our best. These roadblocks will come in the form of fear, doubt, excuses, procrastination, anger, guilt, negative labels, idleness, and other forms of paralysis. As we keep our focus and learn to hurdle these obstacles, we will reach our destination and accomplish our goals. Remember to focus on the prize and don't let anything or anyone distract you from your ultimate reward. We may get knocked down at times, but we never fail unless we quit. So get back up, dust yourself off, and go forward with a relentless determination to succeed. The price to pay is worth the reward, and your focus will give you the strength to live a life of excellence and earn the success you deserve.

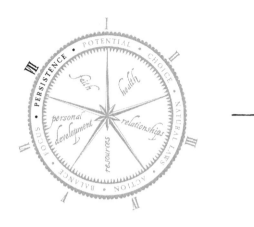

Formula 7:
Breakout

A lifetime commitment to success is found in the pursuit of excellence.

Experience a Breakout

In the years I spent as a financial advisor, I did much stock graph analysis—researching and compiling data that indicated the success of a company. I would often look at a company's fundamental data, such as their earnings over the past five to ten years, their dividend payout, their price-to-earning ratio, their amount of debt, and other data that would be indicative of a successful and profitable company. I would also research the technical data for a company by reviewing the stock price of a company over time, which was represented in the form of a graph. Usually the company graph would take on a particular personality of its own. Some company graphs would go straight up and then straight down. Others would gradually go up to a specific dollar amount and then over time come back to a certain price, establishing a target range. In this manner I came to know common trends that a company would follow. Sometimes the company would develop a trend that was fairly predictable. Over time I would study thousands of graphs and learn how to read these charts so as to make the best decisions for my clients. I wasn't perfect, but I was fairly accurate in predicting potential movement in each company's stock value as it pertained to its graphs.

My wife would laugh at this massive stack of books filled with stock graph analysis, but I really enjoyed studying and gathering information that would increase my expertise as a financial advisor and feed my interest in the stock market. This combination of fundamental and technical data allowed me to assess the viability of a company and make appropriate recommendations for my clients. As a result of much research, I eventually developed a formula that was consistent and profitable.

Over time a stock tends to get what we call a range or pattern in which it consistently trades. A company over the years may range in price from twenty-five to seventy dollars per share. In this instance it becomes common for a stock to have peaks and valleys between these ranges over long periods of time. When a stock moves down toward twenty-five dollars per share, it tends to bounce back up, and when it gets close to its all-time high, it seems to trend down. A *breakout* occurs when a stock is approaching its all-time high, gains momentum, increases in volume, and explodes through its old highs and barriers. Stocks that explode through these barriers oftentimes go on to set incredible gains and increase tremendously in value. Many of the most successful companies have followed this trend and have transcended expectations and realized unfathomable gains and profits. I believe their breakouts were caused by their momentum and a relentless pressure to break through into new ground.

As I noticed these patterns in the stock graphs, I also realized that companies and people go through a similar process of success when they experience a breakout. We as individuals tend to follow a trend in our lives and stay within a range of comfort. Sometimes we fall down a bit and need to pick ourselves up. Other times we are on the verge of greatness but fall back into some of the old habits that curtail our success. If we will go beyond our old limits when we approach our all-time high, we will break out into a new range of success that will facilitate us reaching our potential and allow us to gain tremendous value in life. We will explode through to new frontiers and enjoy an improved quality of life that will be unfathomable. When we experience a breakout in life we begin to live our dreams and enjoy life to its fullest. We start to believe again in our true aspirations and start to gain confidence that these dreams really can be achieved. We start to live rather than just exist.

Range of Limitation

Have you ever felt that your life was getting a little stale? Like you were just going through the motions and each day just blended into the next? If you have ever felt any of these symptoms, you are very normal but are suffering from a range of limitation. This is when we confine ourselves to a specific range of accomplishing and failing, and typically stay within that range. Within this expected range we don't fail too miserably and don't succeed too magnificently either.

Some people's range of limitation has a large variance whereas others' can be quite consistent, but in either case, deep within each one of us is a breakout waiting to happen. Breakouts are fundamental to living at our maximum level of happiness and success.

This range of limitation gets to be comfortable, and we sense that anything that would disrupt that range would cause us pain. Therefore we stay put, oftentimes growing complacent in one or more aspects of our lives, and safely decide this is as good as life gets. We fear the thought of pushing ourselves to a new range because the pain would take us out of our comfort zone and would require greater effort.

A man once said to me that dreams are to be broken and that no one lives the life they intend to. He said that we start off with these great expectations, but as life kicks us in the teeth, we realize that these dreams are unrealistic and can't be achieved. So we take what life gives us and do the best we can. I replied that this is not living at all. I told him that he was subsisting on the bare minimum but that there was so much more he could have if he tried. This man had given up on the chance to really live and accomplish his dreams. His dreams were possible—he just needed to break out of his range of limitation.

We are much more capable than our range of limitation allows us to be, and we have the ability to launch ourselves into greatness. Our limiting range is often a result of feeling inadequate or incapable, so we settle for less than we want and begin to grow complacent with our expectations in every aspect of life. When we do this, our enthusiasm for life and our dreams are extinguished, and we decide that maybe our dreams never could've been a reality after all.

Change the Paradigm

You are capable of realizing your dreams. You can have that relationship you've hoped for with someone who really understands you. You can have that intoxicating love that you have felt at times in your life. You can be the person you want to be and stand strong in your convictions of truth. You can pursue those dreams and passions of life while attending to your responsibilities. You can have the energy and strength you desire from living a healthy life. You can manage your money and time wisely to enjoy the life and values you desire. You can live in this life and not just go through the motions. Life can be exhilarating and exciting and adventurous.

Now, you notice that I never said that life won't deal you a bad hand occasionally. None of us escape the trials and challenges of life, many of which come without warning; however, how we respond to these challenges is up to us. We ultimately decide to either give up on our dreams or allow our challenges to make us even more determined to get there. As we face struggles, which we surely will, we can deepen our resolve and strengthen our determination as we commit to living a life of excellence. Our effort and work will compound the joy we feel as we overcome and persist in our pursuit for success.

Whatever your reality is today, know that you have the ability to change that paradigm to see the world differently if you choose. Your reality is whatever your mind has decided it to be, so if you desire to change your perspective or paradigm, you must change the way you view life. Seeing life as a journey and realizing that the journey will come with some rocks in your path can help your paradigm change. If you embrace the journey and learn from the experiences of life with a determination to be happy, then you will develop a hope and an optimism that will allow you to live life fully and enjoy the journey.

See the Positive

Now some of you may be saying, "It's easy to say that life can be grand and sweet, but that is not reality for me." Your life can be sweet no matter what you are facing. Your days can be happy, and you can reach your dreams if you don't give up hope. In this world we all suffer pain in one form or another. Chances are that those people you think haven't gone through much in their lives have suffered the greatest, but they've discovered how to carry on, lose themselves in the service of others, and still persist in their quest of greatness.

Look at the positive of life and remember the words of Winston Churchill in seeing the opportunity in every difficulty. Always consider the alternative and try to see how your circumstances can make you a better person. You spend the same amount of energy whether you look for the best or the worst, but looking for the worst in every opportunity only distances you from your goal. Spend your energy looking for the positive in life. Rather than finding fault with others, find the good. Rather than seeing all that went wrong in your day, ask yourself what went well. Rather than dwelling on all your shortcomings, look for the blessings. While this perspective may seem trite, consider the alternative. Wouldn't you rather at least give yourself the best chance at happiness and success? Certainly we can't expect that spending our time and energy on negativity will get us anywhere. It won't, and in the end it will leave you only farther from your desired destination.

What you are looking for are powerful results that will allow you to live a life of success and happiness. The only way to achieve lasting success is by implementing correct principles. Spending your time on a positive perspective of life will increase the likelihood of you taking action toward reaching your goals. As you are motivated to succeed, you will be one step closer to living your dreams and realizing your potential.

Clean out the Closet

Have you ever gone through your closet or drawers and realized how much junk you have? And then have you ever experienced the joy of getting rid of all that clutter? Just as many of us store unnecessary clutter in our houses, our lives are also full of similar baggage that is holding us back and weighing us down from becoming our very best. We must eliminate such excess baggage and move forward, free of clutter.

As we rid ourselves of the emotional bricks we've been accruing over the years, we can begin to devote more of our energies and time to attaining our goals. As you clean out your closet of life and get rid of anything that is holding you back, you will begin to live and gain strength and momentum in pursuit of your dreams. When you face a challenge in your day-to-day activities, ask yourself, "Is this moving me closer or farther away from my dreams?" If any of you encounter clutter that moves you farther from the life you desire, eliminate that junk. Keep only those items, thoughts, choices, actions, and words that get you closer to your desired location. This process will help you maintain a clean house of life, and rid you from any unnecessary clutter that would detour your efforts. Whatever it is in life that holds you back from greatness, let it go and move forward in your potential that awaits you.

Endless Potential

Once we break through our old range of comfort and experience a breakout into new ground, the sky will be the limit. We will discover the potential we have within us and desire to maximize our existence. Once we have broken through, we will more clearly realize that our potential is limitless and our minds will be able to expand and visualize to a greater extent the possibilities that await us. You will accomplish things you never imagined possible and enjoy the quality of life you've dreamed of.

Michael Jordan, arguably the best player in professional basketball, understood the breakout theory. When he entered the NBA there had already been many incredible basketball players over the years. These great players were in a league of their own and were all considered to be stars. Jordan didn't set his sites on just being in that range of greatness but instead decided to break through into a new level of play that was never imagined. He didn't want to be one of the best, but rather he set his sights on being the very best. He experienced a breakout as he abandoned his old range of greatness for a range of limitless potential. Jordan reached a level of play in basketball that was never known. Jordan understood how to break out in something he loved and discovered the potential and greatness that he so amply displayed.

We can experience a breakout and discover an entirely new level of commitment to success. We don't have to feel like this is as good as life gets and throw in the towel on the dreams we've had. If we can see it, we can be it. If we will break through our limitation barriers, we will experience a breakout onto new ground, and the sky will be the limit as to what we can achieve. Once at this breakout level of achievement, we must commit to a lifelong path of change and balance and excellence in order to maintain our newfound success. Lasting success is a lifetime commitment to the persistent pursuit of excellence, and if we do this, we will explode past our old expectations and discover a whole different world of possibilities.

Fully Invested

When you have committed to being your best, decide to be fully invested. There is no halfway for a commitment to excellence—either you're committed or you're not. It's as black and white as having a pulse—you either have one or you don't. Being fully invested means that you focus your time, energies, and all you have in you toward reaching your potential, holding nothing back. It means you take advantage of opportunities to learn, grow, and better yourself so that you can be of greater value to others. Breaking through the limiting barriers in your life allows you to fully commit to living your dreams and be fully invested in your energies to do so.

Being fully invested also applies to following correct principles and living our faith. Either we live what we believe or we don't. Can we "kind of" live correct principles and expect to gain the results we desire? When we are fully invested we recognize the laws of correct principles and abide by them. When we fail to do so, we hold back on all we could become, showing that we are not willing to pay the price to merit the prize. As we apply our faith and live correct principles of truth, we discover success and see the unalterable results that come as a result. Decide to be fully invested in your commitment to consistently apply correct principles in your life so that you can gain the ultimate results and success you desire. Don't sell yourself short—be fully invested in your commitment to excellence.

We can also be fully invested when it comes to relationships. This means giving everything we've got to make a relationship successful. That includes sacrificing and forgetting ourselves in the service of those we love, care for, and intend to help. Being fully invested means admitting when you're wrong or saying sorry when you've offended someone. How can we expect to find success in a marriage if we're self-absorbed and only thinking of our own interests? Have you ever been around someone who is constantly saying, "I, I, I . . . It's all about me." Then those people wonder why their life is so unfulfilled.

During college, I asked out a girl who I thought was very beautiful. I picked her up, and we went out for a lovely dinner. I particularly tried to show interest in her and learn what she was about and what her interests were. Well that night my date talked about herself nonstop the entire time. She told me about every accomplishment she'd had since grade school. She mentioned how everyone thought she was beautiful and that there were so many guys who wanted to take her out. I was exhausted by the end of dinner and took her home a little earlier than normal. I figured I could never love this girl as much as she loved herself. Weeks later I saw her in the halls at school, and she asked me if she had said something wrong. To not hurt her feelings I said I'd been busy studying, but I think she understood.

Whether you are making new acquaintances, catching up with your spouse, or visiting with friends, be "fully invested" by taking an interest in others. Make your conversation more about them than about you. You will notice that people will want to be around you more, and you will gain a greater bond with those who are close to you. Taking an interest in others shows your concern for them and develops a greater, longer-lasting relationship.

This same rule applies in business relationships. If the person you're doing business with only steers things to their advantage, chances are you will not be doing business too much longer. When it comes to relationships, whether business or personal, we must have a win-win mentality. Add value to the relationships around you and don't always think, "What's in it for me?"

You can get to know a lot about a person by the way they apply the 7th M&M Rule. Let me explain. If you had seven M&M's and were splitting them with another individual, how would you divide the candies? Would you keep four and give the other person three, or would you keep three and give up the fourth . . . or would you say, "What M&M's?" Think of family members or people you do business with. Can you easily tell what they would do in a similar situation?

Everyone wants to do business with a person who is willing to give up the seventh M&M. This simple, yet effective tool can tell a lot about the person you are dealing with. I have many good relationships with others who would give you the seventh M&M every time. These people are content with three candies and understand that when you give more than you receive, the reward comes back to you in many more ways. When you know someone else received the tie-breaking prize, you feel good that they feel good, and that contentment is a reward in and of itself. On the contrary, when we deal with others who take the seventh M&M and always have to get an advantage, we are less comfortable and less likely to want to work or interact with them.

I had a business partner who was so fair, he would neither give you the seventh M&M nor keep it for himself—he would divide it right down the middle. I appreciated his exactness and the comfort of knowing that at least he was honest. I've also had other partners who would give you the extra prize, regardless, because if you were happy, they were happier.

I joke about this rule to a degree, but I can usually tell from my relationships with others which types of friends and business associates add value to life and understand the formula for a positive, meaningful relationship. The 7th M&M Rule should not be a premise for divorce or breaking off a large company contract; however, it can be a fun and effective tool in human interaction. The next time someone asks you to split up the M&M's, be careful and make sure you give up the seventh!

As you may have gathered by now, being "fully invested," means giving our best in whatever aspect of life we are focusing on at that time. Being fully invested allows us to break out into new ground and achieve heights we've never seen before. We can be fully invested with our faith, relationships, personal development, health, and resources (time and money). Being "fully invested" commits us to excellence in each of these values and strengthens our resolve to take action. As we are fully invested, we will breakout of our limiting barriers, and be successful in obtaining real results in our lives. These results will give us great satisfaction and deepen our purpose and resolve to live our greatest dreams.

Shatter the Glass

As we go through life, a ceiling of expectation tends to form above us and puts a cap on our performance. This ceiling can become a barrier that traps us in a life of mediocrity and complacency. It almost becomes like glass, showing us the reflection of our potential, but then we sometimes lack the strength and resolve to crack through. The only way we can get past this barrier is to shatter the glass. Just like a successful stock, we must gain momentum and reach for a higher level of results that will set a new precedence for our lives.

Many times when we are so close to reaching this glass ceiling, we meet resistance head-on. The resistance stifles our progress, and we slip back into our comfort zone, fearing that the price to pay by shattering the glass may be too painful. This resistance keeps us from our greatest potential, and if we could just get the strength to shatter this ceiling, there would be untold rewards and greatness waiting for us. Determine that you will not just break through the glass but that you will shatter that ceiling and explode through to achieve your greatest potential. Decide that there is no resistance too great to hold you within the glass ceiling. You will not be stifled.

Remember the stock charts I described earlier? Many stocks would reach their new high but would fall back into the range of comfort and settle for the same old pattern that had been in place for some time. In order for a stock to break into new ground, it had to shatter through the old high with huge volume to form a new pattern of expectation. When a company was able to shatter through the old range, it went on to extraordinary potential and growth, reaching new heights never before achieved.

We too can shatter through our old highs and reach for new potential and greatness. Decide that you will not settle for mediocrity in your life, but instead will shatter through your old limitations and explode to new levels and greatness. Start today, no matter where you are, and make a commitment to excellence. Determine to be your best at all times, in all places, and under any circumstances. Don't settle for "this is as good as life gets." Break the old record in your mental jukebox and burn a new CD for life. Decide to live the life you've dreamed of and settle for nothing less.

Life can weigh us down at times. We all suffer and succumb to the pressures and resistance of life; however, we have a say in the matter. Ultimately we are the ones who determine how our story will end. We are the authors of our lives and have the liberty to script this experience how we desire—we don't need to settle. We can break out of our old range of comfort and explode through to a level of greatness we have never known. The future and opportunity are right before us and are waiting. Live the life you intended and explode through to greatness.

Recap: Into a Range of Greatness

Just like company stocks, most of us as individuals rise and fall within comfortable ranges of minute successes and insignificant failures, afraid to breakout and explode through the ceiling to unimaginable success. The breakout principle separates good from great. It is that little extra push that allows us to break through the roadblocks to success and achieve our ultimate potential in life. Oftentimes we settle for mediocrity and even convince ourselves that this is as good as it gets. We lull ourselves into a range of comfort and little risk or effort when deep inside we know there is more in store for us.

Decide now that you will not settle for a life of mediocrity. Change your paradigm so that you see and think positively, strengthening your resolve that nothing can keep you from achieving your dreams. There will be times when life knocks you to the ground and even drags you a bit. When this happens, get up. Everyone gets knocked down, but it's those who get up that win. Get up no matter what life throws at you and no matter how hard life may seem. When life throws you a curve ball, respond by knocking it clear out of the park.

As we take responsibility for our choices and commit to excellence no matter our circumstances, we place ourselves on a path that unlocks the potential within us. We become fully invested in going after our dreams—no holding back, no excuses—and confidently expect to see the results we desire. As we tap into the potential that is within us and correctly apply true principles, we will experience an amazing breakout from the old range and enjoy the success and happiness that come from living the fullness of life.

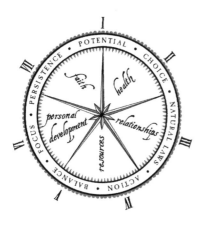

Blueprint for Success

It's Time to Begin

Having determined that our five core values are faith, relationships, personal development, health, and resources (time and money), we now solidify their significance in our lives by condensing our wants into a blueprint for success. Look around you and assess if we could use a blueprint of core values to guide our decisions. In the world today, we are witnessing a record number of broken relationships, depression, suicide, health issues, and financial turmoil. There is no question that we all need a personalized blueprint to keep us focused on our goals and help us implement formulas for success into our everyday lives.

This blueprint of correct principles will act as a map to remind us of our goals and priorities. You are free to customize your blueprint as long as it includes the following: (1) what your goals are, (2) why they are important to you, (3) how you're going to accomplish them, and (4) when you will make time for them during your week. By establishing set guidelines to accomplish our goals, we are more prepared to steer clear of unnecessary detours and avoid time-robbing pitfalls. When we implement all of the action points found in this book and apply the Seven Formulas for Success to our lives, we will be able to pick up wherever we are and start down the road to success.

When we truly understand that the common denominators for success stem from obedience to certain natural laws and that there is no way around it, we will begin to embrace these laws and tap into the reservoir of unlimited potential that comes through their proper application. I remember sitting in high school biology and feeling somewhat clever because a friend and I had devised a system to check each other's test answers based on a signal system. For a multiple-choice test, A was coughing, B was touching your nose, C was tying your shoe, and D was scratching your knee. While we thought we had broken the barrier of genius and had certainly opened up a funnel of incredible opportunity, I later realized that I had only cheated myself. Yes, we enjoyed temporary stardom among our fellow peers and a reprieve of studying, but I clearly shorted myself of the opportunity to truly learn.

Some may ask, "Is that so bad?" As I mentioned earlier, you can't get long-lasting results by going against the system; it will never work. I may have temporarily had an illusion of success, but it was based on an incorrect principle of cheating. While this may sound trivial, it illustrates the point that rules are set up for our success and safety, and as we tap into their correct application, we will merit positive results. My teacher eventually called me in after she found it quite a coincidence that my answers and those of my friend were identical. She couldn't explain it, considering my friend and I sat on opposite sides of the room. I was embarrassed and knew that I had tried to gain a positive result from a negative application of a principle. This will never work, and the system will always claim its victim.

With consistent application, the Seven Formulas for Success can unlock the barriers that are keeping you from reaching your full potential. Once you learn these seven formulas, you will be able to apply them to your blueprint for success to reaffirm your core values. With this newfound knowledge and confidence, you will be ready to move forward and reach your ultimate potential. Put the past in perspective and learn from it; visualize the future ahead and prepare for it; and focus on the present and live it!

Action Points of the Seven Universal Formulas

Throughout the Seven Formulas for Success I included various action points—things you can physically do to achieve your life goals. Each of these tasks belongs in your blueprint for success so that you clearly know what it will take to reach your goal. Before creating your blueprint, consider removing yourself from distractions and going somewhere peaceful where you can seriously consider what you want out of life. This always helps me so that I'm prepared to crystallize my thoughts on paper. The more solid you are in your desires, the more committed you will be to creating a logical blueprint for success, complete with your own to-do lists and short- and long-term goals. To

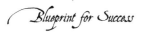

help you know what you can now do to create your blueprint for success and better visualize these action points, I've listed them here with brief explanations.

As If Principle

Write down your desires as if you had already accomplished them. So, for example, you could write down, "I am productive and focus 100 percent on the task before me." The As If Principle states that all things you want in life must be based on correct principles and that proper application of these principles will produce the results you desire. For this principle to work—and for not only your brain to get in the habit of believing this but also for your body to follow through on these thoughts—you must base your thoughts, words, and actions on correct principles. So determine who you want to be and what you want to accomplish, and then create your list of positive affirmations to put the As If Principle to the test.

Universal Laws

Another action point to help you establish a blueprint is to observe the world and start to notice that everything follows natural laws. These universal laws keep us safe, provide us with freedom, and are found in our very surroundings, such as in the orbit of the earth, on speed limit signs, and even in the way we breathe. Knowing that there is an order to life, we can tap into those laws that govern success in the areas that matter most to us. We can develop balance in our five core values of faith, relationships, personal development, health, and resources as we learn the common denominators for total success—the seven formulas presented in this book. Once we understand that all things are set up in this manner, we can begin to implement natural laws for our own success.

One time when I went bodysurfing as a teenager, I noticed a red flag indicating that there was a strong undercurrent. I should have recognized the potential consequences of ignoring that warning, but I thought I was smarter and headed into the ocean with my brother. We were the only ones in the water—warning sign number two. As we finished bodysurfing, we started to make our way to shore but quickly realized that we couldn't get back in. We started to get extremely tired, and before we knew it there was a rescue team on shore, telling us to get out of the water. We were caught in the severe undercurrent we'd been warned of by the red flag. My muscles started to cramp, and I knew my brother and I would be in serious trouble if we didn't get out soon. The lifeguards instructed us to swim down the shoreline, around the current, and then back in to shore. I was on my last leg as I came crawling up the beach.

I learned a valuable lesson that day: when we follow the rules and obey the laws, we are free. Over the years you may have recognized valuable lessons in your own life but never equated them to universal laws. But now you know what to look for and how to interpret your experiences to increase your ability to succeed in life. Apply these lessons to your blueprint for success to be even more effective in reaching your goals.

Success Journal

To help you get the hang of recognizing universal laws and true principles, keep a success journal. Write down what works in

life as well as what doesn't work to then notice patterns and to better understand the law. Recording your findings will give you strength in overcoming opposition and help you clearly see what you are doing right and what you can improve. In a success journal you can openly express yourself, recording your thoughts on how to apply your newfound knowledge to your personal goals. These principles of success cover many aspects of life, including interpersonal communication, effective time management, proper use of money, attributes of a successful person, formulas for successful weight loss, etc. Recording your findings can help you be a more effective goal planner, solidify your ideas, and pull knowledge from life experiences to then turn it into wisdom. Keeping a success journal will help you create a personalized blueprint for success that is based on your own life experiences.

WBDA Principle

The WBDA Principle stands for: "Want it. Believe it. Do it. Achieve it." We can use this natural law to pursue our greatest desires in life. Each of these four steps builds upon the other until we have achieved our goal.

First we must identify what we really want out of life. These wants are derived from our core values, which include faith, relationships, personal development, health, and resources, and must be based on correct principles. To get to the core of our real desires, we need to peel back our own personal layers as you would an onion. Then and only then will we get down to those values and goals that have greatest significance in our lives.

Second we must believe that we can obtain the desires of our heart. In order to truly believe in ourselves, we must break down the limitation barriers and increase our imagination of what is possible. Believing means to visualize ourselves accomplishing our greatest desires. Surrounding ourselves with positive influences and exercising the As If Principle will strengthen our ability to believe and give us the necessary motivation to take action.

Once we identify our real wants and believe that these desires are possible, we must put together a plan of action, or a to-do list, that will make these dreams a reality. This to-do list is comprised of all the necessary steps that we must take to realize our short- and long-term goals. We need a specific plan in order to remain motivated and follow through with accomplishing our dreams.

Finally, after we've put a plan of action in place, we must execute the plan. A dream without execution is just a dream, but a dream with action becomes a reality. Our ability to execute a plan is crucial in completing this process. Oftentimes we face roadblocks that test our will and our resolve, but when we execute despite roadblocks, we break out from a life of mediocrity into a life of greatness.

As you include all of these action points in your blueprint for success and personalize them, it will be clear what you must do each day to make your dreams a reality. The better you know what you want, the more committed you'll be to follow through on the goals you've outlined in your blueprint for success. There is nothing that can stand in your way, not even you!

Review of the Seven Formulas for Success

Formula 1: *Within each of us lies unlimited potential. The only limitations in life are those we place upon ourselves.*

Each of us has unlimited potential. We are hindered only by our own doubts and fears. With confidence and direction, we can achieve whatever we set our minds to, so dream big. Enlarge your vision of what is possible; determine what you need to do to accomplish your dreams; surround yourself with positive influences that motivate you to be your best; and rise to that level of greatness you're seeking.

Formula 2: *Success is not a matter of chance but a matter of choice.*

Take charge of your life by taking charge of your choices. Every day you make decisions that either bring you closer to reaching your dreams or take you farther away. No matter what life has dealt you, no matter what circumstances you have grown up in, no matter where you have been, you are not a victim of your circumstances. You may not have control over what life sends your way, but you always have the power to choose your reaction. Don't make excuses for failure, but rather choose to succeed and to take full responsibility for your destination in life.

Formula 3: *Results stem from natural laws adhered to or broken.*

Success in life follows a formula: in order to gain our desired results, we need to learn the laws and then abide by their rules. Every time we follow a formula for success, it yields a reward; every time we disobey, it yields a consequence. The laws will not be fooled. There are no shortcuts to obtaining the reward, and when we try to trick the system, we lose. By learning the formulas to success and obeying them, we can achieve those rewards that unlock our true potential. Paying the price is the cost of admission to realizing our dreams, and there is no other way around it.

Formula 4: *Wisdom is knowledge applied.*

The key ingredient to making a dream a reality is action. When we take action we demonstrate faith that positive results will come when we pay the price. Because wisdom is knowledge applied, taking action literally moves us beyond mere knowledge into the realm of wisdom and then propels us toward our intended results. The WBDA Principle is one such universal law that explains how every success comes from applying knowledge through action. This law tells us that to reach our goal we have to (1) want it bad enough, (2) believe we can accomplish it, (3) do something by creating a plan, and then (4) achieve our goal by executing that plan. As students for life, we are constantly adding to our knowledge and moving forward to determine what it is we want in life, why we want it, how we're going to get it, and when we will devote time to getting it. As we put all of these pieces in place,

following the natural laws we've observed and applying our knowledge, we will be successful.

Formula 5: *Real success is the consistent application of correct principles in every aspect of life.*

Establishing balance is a necessary element of a successful life. Just as a chair missing a leg is off balance, we cannot find stability without achieving success in all five of the core values—faith, relationships, personal development, health, and resources. A deficit in any one of these areas will produce catastrophic results in our overall satisfaction in life. The only way to have total fulfillment is to consciously balance our lives and prioritize our core values. When we are balanced, we avoid many pitfalls of life that come from being overly consumed in just one area. Through the correct application of universal formulas we can balance our spiritual, physical, mental, emotional, social, financial, and personal needs, and enjoy the fullness of life.

Formula 6: *Focus is achieved as we overcome roadblocks to success.*

Life will inevitably come with its share of challenges. These roadblocks to success come in the form of fear, doubt, excuses, procrastination, and other paralyzing obstacles. All of these hurdles share one crippling component: they suspend action and paralyze progress. We must recognize when these challenges come our way and know that their intent is to thwart our efforts. By focusing on our core values and goals, we can remain diligent to our purpose and constant in our mission. Learn from your mistakes to prepare for the future and to live a more productive today. Let your challenges make you even more determined to realize your goals and to live your dreams. Overcome roadblocks to success by staying focused on your dream and pursuing your potential with a relentless determination no matter what stands in your way.

Formula 7: *A lifetime commitment to success is found in the persistent pursuit of excellence.*

Each of us has a range of comfort in life that we tend to stay in. Going outside of our comfort zone often scares us, and that fear limits what we are capable of. In order to elevate ourselves to an even higher level of greatness, we must experience a breakout from the old range of comfort and explode into a level of ultimate success. This breakout requires us to be fully invested with intense determination and momentum to shatter the glass ceiling that has restricted us all these years. Once you shatter this barrier, you will see amazing results and finally start living your life. Don't settle for a life of mediocrity or complacency, but commit yourself to a life of excellence. Determine to be your best at all times, in all places, and under any circumstance. Live your life by correct principles and remain firm despite the distractions that may surround you. As you commit your life to excellence, you will become a participant rather than just an observer.

Recap: The Only Way to True Success

Each of us has dreams we want to realize, and after reading this book, each of us now knows the common denominators

to achieving greatness and breaking through the roadblocks of life. Everyone who has ever truly succeeded in this world has followed the seven formulas laid out in this book—they are universal principles that know no boundaries of race, gender, religion, or culture. These universal laws teach us that it is impossible to reach our dreams while doing nothing, no matter how fabulous and fool-proof the latest trend diet or get-rich-quick scheme may sound. Instead of focusing on how little you can do to reach your goal, focus on what is required of you to reach your greatest dreams and enjoy lasting results. Now is the time to take control of your life and create your own blueprint for success.

Dare to live your dreams by applying these seven universal formulas to your life. Seek to better recognize the natural laws all around you that govern this universe so that you can tap into their power. Break out of the old mold and reach for the potential that is within you. What do you have to lose? Nothing. But you have everything to gain. Invest yourself in this life, realize your limitless capacity to succeed, and help others do the same. As you do so, you will find that this life is an amazing journey and that lifelong dreams really can come true.

Acknowledgments

Writing this book has been a personal quest and dream of mine for more than twenty years. During this time I've dedicated countless hours to research, observation, thought, and experience in order to identify the common denominators for total success in life. The content of this book is a result of a lifetime of learning, and I would like to acknowledge some of the people who have influenced this passion and have contributed to the completion of this book.

I want to thank my parents for teaching me principles of success from an early age and for instilling in me a confidence that I could accomplish anything I set my mind to.

I want to express my love and appreciation to my wife, Rebecca, and our four children. Their support and example are a great inspiration to me.

I also want to thank my editor, Katie Newbold, for believing in this book and for devoting countless hours of time and energy in its completion. Her dedication and commitment made this book possible.

About the Author

After graduating from Brigham Young University in psychology, Kenny Anderson began his career as a financial advisor, consulting individuals and companies throughout the U.S. for nearly a decade. As an entrepreneur, Anderson founded several businesses. Among these business ventures was the start of his own development company, where Anderson was responsible for more than one hundred million dollars in real estate transactions during his eight years in the industry. Anderson also invented and patented an idea for an athletic shoe, which later evolved into his company Leaper Footwear, LLC. Since 1998 Leaper has licensed its patent to some of the largest companies in the world.

As an author, Anderson now spends his time consulting and speaking about how to apply the Seven Formulas for Success to gain a fulfilling life. He is dedicated to helping individuals and companies achieve successful results, maintain a healthy balance to life, and find their unlimited potential.